Katherine Mansfield's Fiction

Katherine Mansfield's Fiction

Patrick D. Morrow

Bowling Green State University Popular Press
Bowling Green, OH 43403

To and for Iokeiti, my Sleepy Jean

Contents

Contents

Acknowledgements

Oh sure, I had read a a couple of KM short stories for my Ph D. comps, and later, I taught a couple more of her stories. But I really had no idea of what Katherine Mansfield was about until I went to New Zealand. Thus, I owe a great deal to the Fulbright Program for sending me twice to the South Pacific. While there, I came under the tutelage of Dr. Cherry Hankin, the Mansfield expert at the University of Canterbury. We certainly do not always agree, but she guides this eager student with a velvet hand. In Wellington, where there was a great deal of interest in Mansfield when I was there in 1989, I would like to thank several people, particularly the official and the unofficial curators of the Mansfield House on 25 Tinakori Road. My primary research was made possible through the kind assistance of the Alexander Turnbull Library, now part of the National Library of New Zealand in Wellington. I also would like to thank Brian Opie, Roger Robinson, and especially David Dowling for their help.

Stateside, I owe a lot of gratitude to Dr. Bert Hitchcock, former Head of the English Department at Auburn, for being a warm, understanding and reliable friend, who made it possible for me to include a significant amount of KM in two courses. I also owe a lot to the following colleagues, friends, and students: Cheryl Bailey, Scott Boozer, Mary Beth Bridges, Barbara Gellert, JoLee Gibbons, John Grimmett, Gwen Noles, Mary Rohrberger, Lee Anna Sellers, Sarah Webb and Mark Willis. I would like to thank Garland Press for allowing me to reprint parts of "Katherine Mansfield: The Idea of the Perfect Short Story," an article I did for them in 1989. Samantha Gill, Lea Seaborn and Linda DeWitt of War Eagle Typing did the typing from a very scarred and edited manuscript.

For the research apparatus, I have used an adaptation of the most recent *MLA Handbook*. For all substantial KM direct quotations in the text, a page number appears in parentheses directly after the quote. All quotes from Mansfield's stories come from the reliable and quite available editions by The Ecco Press (New York) called *The Short Stories of Katherine Mansfield.* Several chapters herein have an additional "Sources" page. By using this page, retrieving my other sources should be clear and easy.

It is most appropriate that the Popular Press of Bowling Green State University has agreed to publish this book because it is such a direct vindication of its former Director, Ray B. Browne. Or, as the late James W. Hall, one of my graduate school mentors was want to say, "nothing fails like success." Katherine Mansfield tried as hard as she could to be the consummate writer. She certainly felt that to be abrasive was to be Modern. Her stories try to be innovative, often excoriating protests, almost always difficult to grasp, very complicated, and typically attempts at virtuoso performances. She desperately wished to be innovative and destructive of Victorian conformism. Or, as we say in Dixie, she had no intention at all of being NICE. But despite her hostility and sarcasm, she wanted people to purchase and read these excursions into complexity, honesty, and sometimes depravity. In other words, she was an elite Modernist.

Well, it has been almost 70 years since she died; we have moved from Modernism into Post-modernism; and Katherine Mansfield is the one New Zealand writer whose name most literate people recognize. With the passage of time comes an increase in familiarity. Or, to paraphrase John Cawelti in *Adventure, Mystery, and Romance*, invention *becomes* convention. That KM would eventually become a minor literary industry, and—dear God!—a *popular* writer, subject to being frequently anthologized, I believe would have made Mansfield blush with pride and be quite ashamed. But as Dr. Browne has taught us, popularity depends little on quality (however we may wish to determine what that is), but on how audience values spin.

I very much appreciate the endurance and patience of my family during the writing of this book. To and for my wife, Dr. Joyce Rothschild, what else is there to say except *mange tak*? However, assistance can only take one so far, and for the inadequacies and errors in *Katherine Mansfield's Fiction*, I take full responsibility.

The Plan of This Book

While Katherine Mansfield has been very lucky to have had several first rate biographers, in my opinion not anywhere near enough exact and in depth literary criticism on her individual stories is available. Therefore, the mission of this volume is to provide many specific interpretations for KM's many stories. Not every story Katherine wrote is considered, but I hope and trust that enough representative examples from all five of her books are explicated so that the reader of this book will come away from it with a greatly increased understanding of what and how much Mansfield accomplished as a writer of short fiction.

Ironically, the first chapter is about a biographical issue that has not received enough discussion. Despite the substantial and very skillful biographical work on Mansfield by Antony Alpers, Saralyn Daly, Jeffrey Meyers, Claire Tomalin, and others, Mansfield's veritable obsession with moving needs more consideration. This is an especially important issue because it relates so much to her career as a creative writer. The second chapter uses three recent literary critics in an attempt to establish some basic ground rules with KM's fiction. Only by applying some critical approaches can we really distinguish Mansfield's depth and complexity as a writer of short fiction. The three critics I use are Mieke Bal, a Dutch feminist critic who writes about narratology; then M.H. Short, who writes about types of indirect discourse in *Language and Literature*; and finally, Seymour Chatman who writes in *Story and Discourse* about problems and issues that arise when narration gives way to non-narration in a story.

Then, I consider Mansfield's stories book by book. She is a really uneven writer, so that some of her most accomplished stories come very early, and some of her weakest stories are written very late. This sense of being inconsistent and uneven adds to both the problems and excitement of reading Katherine Mansfield. She wrote three volumes of short stories, and her

1

husband, editor John M. Murry, edited two other volumes of her stories. From almost any perspective a reader wishes to consider, each volume has stories of outstanding quality, and each volume has stories of somewhat lesser competence.

The concluding chapter of the text posits Mansfield against several other, mostly British, writers. Anton Chekhov is included because he was so influential to British Moderns, and he has special importance for Mansfield, not only because of his very clear influence on her, but also because of the charge rendered against KM because of her plagiarizing a Chekhov story. To encounter more information on this issue, I recommend that the reader see what Alpers has to say in *Katherine Mansfield, A Biography* (375 to 421), or consider Claire Tomalin's reaction to this issue in *Katherine Mansfield: A Secret Life* (125 to 131). Besides Chekhov and KM compared, I have made brief but pointed comparisons of KM with Elizabeth Bowen, James Joyce, D.H. Lawrence, Jean Rhys and Virginia Woolf. A select bibliography and an index conclude this volume.

This is not an easy book to read. If such had been my intention, it would have been quite simple to pick out my own personal favorites among KM's 88 stories, and then come up with a thesis and some theoretical criticism about why this view of mine "has substantial merit." The book would also have been shorter. Instead, what I have tried to do with this book is give the reader an idea and a feeling for the kinds of textures and issues that KM stories have. In order to realize at least somewhat the types of artistry Mansfield could produce, the informed reader needs to be aware of many different settings, conflicts, and concerns that KM exhibited in her writing. While conclusions and estimations sound entirely too much like cocktail party talk, a more complete understanding of the many ways in which Mansfield was such an accomplished writer of short fiction surely is reward worthy of some real attention and effort.

Basic KM Biography

(Katherine Mansfield used so many pseudonyms that KM is a standard reference to her.) KM was the third daughter of an overbearing colonial father and a prim and proper mother who left the loving of her children to her own mother. Of course, KM's family was actually not so cut and dried; there existed complex relationships between the four Beauchamp daughters, their only brother, their parents, their grandmother and their mother's sister. It is known that KM wanted desperately to leave her family and New Zealand, to travel, to be independent even from those people she loved dearly, like her brother, Leslie. KM was sent with her sisters to a finishing school in London in 1903, but this did not make her a cultured, quiet and male-supportive young lady; rather, KM was already a writer, and in 1908, she returned to New Zealand and persuaded her father to let her live in England on a yearly allowance of £100.

Katherine arrived back in London shortly before her 20th birthday. The first three years of her independence was the most disordered time of her life; her own letters and journals are fragmentary, and there is little positive information about this period. KM had studied music as a girl, and had played the cello; information about her expertise in this field is, typical of KM's life, surprisingly scarce. In 1908-09, KM renewed her friendship with Arnold Trowell, a young cellist, and fell in love with his brother, Garnet. KM had previous affairs, sexual experiences of some kind, with young men and women in New Zealand, but little is known about these relationships; they were, of course, kept quiet, being decidedly improper conduct for a well-off young lady of Victorian upbringing. Katherine wanted to try out her new independence from this kind of upbringing, and she became pregnant as a result, either by Garnet or someone else, either before or after her one day's marriage to George Bowden. KM traveled to Bavaria where she miscarried, and where she wrote *In a German Pension*, her first collection of short stories. There were

3

several other love affairs during this time and perhaps a second pregnancy terminated in either miscarriage or abortion.

KM met John Middleton Murry in 1911. They became lovers, then lived together, then co-edited a literary periodical called *Rhythm*, which Murry had begun editing not long before. KM's publisher offered to act as publisher of *Rhythm*, but he went bankrupt almost immediately, leaving both Murry's magazine and KM's possibilities for literary fame in financial difficulties. The couple continued the magazine for a while, however, calling it *The Blue Review*. During the summer of 1913, KM and Murry stayed together only on weekends; these week-long separations resulted in volumes of letters which have been made to seem the record of one of the world's most beautiful love affairs. Actually, between 1911 and 1918, when KM's divorce from her first husband came through and she could marry Murry, the relationship between Murry and KM covered a veritable spectrum of feeling–from intense love to hostile estrangement. Murry was a man very much like KM's father. He loved KM, but he hovered as well, constricting her, and refusing to accept her as a whole person, equal to himself. Murry's love was exciting to KM, but she needed to be recognized as an individual. Her battle with recurring illness began in 1914 with her first attack of pleurisy, and illness strengthened KM's desire for independence. In future years, when KM was most dependent on others, these would be the times when she most wanted to function alone.

Katherine had, even while she was with Murry, an existence apart from him. She went to France as an escape from Murry's hovering, and while there had an affair with Francis Carco. When KM returned to Murry, she entered into a very productive period of writing, but this literary development was stopped cold for a time by her beloved brother's 1915 death from a training accident in France. KM responded to her brother's death with an intense hysteria, but she gradually overcame the trauma and began writing again. She and Murry were still waiting for KM's divorce to come through, but Leslie's death and Murry's suffocating protection combined to kill her desire for Murry. She wanted him for a while as a kind of surrogate brother, but Katherine's character was too attuned to actuality for playing this game very long.

In 1917, KM suffered from a second attack of pleurisy and

journeyed to the south of France to escape the English winter and, again, Murry's attentions. Murry would not or could not leave his war work in London, so KM traveled alone. She did not desire his company, perhaps, but Murry's priorities here caused a major break in their still friendly relationship. When KM was diagnosed as having tuberculosis, she was joined by her old friend Ida Baker (known as LM). Ida, like Murry, hovered over KM. Ironically, it was only a short time later that KM's divorce was settled, and she returned with Ida to London to marry Murry.

KM struggled to cross France and after three weeks arrived in England; she married Murry in May 1918. Mansfield no longer had the financial worries with which she and Murry had been plagued since the beginning of their relationship. Murry now had a good income from editing, but KM was not particularly productive in the months after she married Murry. She was preoccupied with her illness and could not seem to force herself to write short stories, although she did write a good deal in her journals. KM was frightened of dying and refused to believe the doctors who gave her only two or three years to live. It was not until KM recognized that her death was only a matter of time that she began both to write incessantly and to search frantically for a cure.

Moving restlessly from place to place, sometimes accompanied by Murry or LM and sometimes not, Katherine wrote some of her best work. She worked constantly, attempting to create literature by which she would be remembered. In October 1922, she joined the Gurdjeff Institute near Paris in a last desperate attempt to cure herself, and she lived there for three months. KM wrote to Murry at the end of December, asking him to come visit her in early January. He came, and KM died a few hours later, on January 9, 1923.

While it is undeniably true that KM's major contribution to literature has been and will continue to be regarded as her five volumes of carefully and innovatively complex short fiction, she did some distinctive other writing as well. Mainly through the connection and support of her husband, editor John Middleton Murry, Mansfield produced a considerable number of literary essays and reviews. Besides loving to perform dramas, she also wrote a number of her own theatrical *jeu d'esprits*. Motivated by rage and the desire for experimentation with language and form,

Mansfield over her tragically few creative years wrote a surprisingly substantial amount of poetry. According to Cherry A. Hankin, the Mansfield expert who edited the moving and extensive *Letters Between Katherine and John Middleton Murry*, this correspondence: "In a sense...is the novel she never wrote" (Hankin 2). In addition, Mansfield produced that anomaly of prose called *The Urewera Journal.*

KM's short stories are complex, so much so that many people avoid the hidden agendas by reading her stories from their own agendas, and thus on a very superficial level. Other people avoid Mansfield's work entirely, refusing to be bothered with mere short stories. A superficial reading of Mansfield's stories is unsatisfactory because it overlooks KM's patterns, her love of words and her purposes in writing. To avoid Mansfield's fiction is to miss a fine author's work; Mansfield's stories are all the more striking because they hit hard, then are gone. A KM novel would perhaps be too violently fine to bear, or perhaps Mansfield's cutting technique would be ruined in a novel.

In fact, KM did not need to write a novel. She was busy experimenting with the idea of the perfect short story, trying to capture perfection over and over again, and different each time. Mansfield composed with language, played music and painted pictures with her words, then crushed the art with the real. Mansfield demands, then almost abuses, the active reader; the author's words are beautiful, but their meaning cuts and leaves one cold.

Because KM's stories are complex, one cannot afford to ignore any aspect of their meaning. Mansfield uses watercolor language to paint pictures of anguish, cruelty, ugliness. One must examine the patterns which run through Mansfield's stories, without being held too long in the author's language. Several patterns of character and theme appear: experiences of the family, communication gaps in marriage and in romantic relationships, class distinctions, the male as simultaneously domineering and weak, the female as victim but deserving of her punishment because she allows herself to be victimized and the idea of lying. These patterns relate closely to KM's life, but Mansfield's stories are not simply illustrations of her life. Mansfield's thoughts and feelings, coming from her experiences, gave her material to work with, but the stories were created in her imagination. To hone in on one character to be KM neglects the fact that Mansfield created all her characters and their thoughts.

Mansfield's stories are not all alike. Themes recur, but these themes vary in how they are presented. Some stories are schematic; they may serve as warnings or may make specific points. Other stories require more probing on the reader's part; they are full of hidden meanings as forceful as the thoughts expressed in the schematic stories, but which must be decoded before the reader is hit. Because Mansfield wrote different kinds of stories, some people feel that her experimentation kept her from developing a particular style. KM did have a style, but that style was never stagnation. Her style was achieved in her words, in her approach to varied themes and in her prevailing ambition—to create the perfect short story. Mansfield's several unfinished stories have a gothic and surrealistic dimension. It is haunting to realize that the answer to the question "what will happen next and why" shall eternally evade the KM reader.

With Mansfield's seemingly endless masques, lies, remarkable relationships with so many remarkable people, her wildly individual combination of colonialism and European experiences, plus her unusual reactions to her severe health crisis, a great deal of attention has been paid to her biography. True, she led an extraordinarily creative and fascinating life. Yes, KM was bisexual, and yes, she possibly had a venereal disease, in addition to tuberculosis. But what a Mansfield bibliography quickly reveals is the sketchy amount of understanding and explication of her literary work currently available. While Mansfield's life has been pretty thoroughly explored, with Mansfield's writing, there is still much to say.

Chapter One
Shifting House with Kass

Katherine Mansfield's life—34 brief, intense years—was spent in a state of perpetual motion. Born in Wellington, New Zealand on 14 October 1888, she began moving almost immediately. Her family left their home for the first time in 1893, moving to Karori (on the outskirts of Wellington). As though the tone was set, she began a life of flux. In 1903, at the age of 15, she went to London to attend Queen's College. From the time she finished school there in 1906 until her death on 9 January 1923, she moved approximately 72 times. Seventy-two moves in 33 years—a startling number of adjustments when one considers the nature of her life. She was stricken with some sort of venereal disease at about age 22, and then had to combat the horrid effects of a misguided operation designed to "cure" her illness. She developed pleurisy and suffered constant attacks of coughing punctuated by intense fevers. She developed tuberculosis and lived from moment to moment—never knowing when she might die. Yet, in spite of these problems and the resulting physical and emotional pain she lived with, she constantly moved—never once standing still during her life. *Why? Why* did Mansfield feel driven to move continually? *What* was it exactly that she was so desperately hoping to find? In this chapter, I will examine these issues and attempt to provide an explanation of her reasons for remaining in constant motion throughout her brief existence.

Katherine Mansfield never seemed to be able to live in one place for very long. With her family in New Zealand, Mansfield must have felt terribly suffocated, especially after she had returned from school in London, her dreams and ambitions, her very self, stifled and repressed. This feeling of suffocation seems to have hounded Mansfield for the rest of her life, constantly at the back of her mind. She always seemed to be searching for something more, trying to be someone better. When Mansfield moved away from

8

the shelter of her parents for good in 1908, at the age of 20, she began the series of moves that would last until she died in 1923.

Katherine Mansfield began her life as an outsider within her own family. Her family—always concerned with the correct socially acceptable existence—made Katherine feel different. She was introverted, sensitive, intense and saw their style of living as superficial and confining, and she did not care to emulate it. In effect, they required her to efface herself and don an acceptable mask for their benefit. Unhappy with the false, social mask she was required to wear, she sought an existence in which prescribed roles and boundaries were not a requirement. But consequently her recognition of this requirement made the issue dominate in her life. She refused to wear socially prescribed masks—instead she created her own roles, not to suit society, but to establish and maintain control. "What she wanted was the power to control her own life without being held in any web of convention" (Tomalin 45). Continually moving gave her the opportunity to re-create herself, taking on the identity that would give her the most control—power over situations and people. Never exposing herself or making herself vulnerable gave her this ability. "In her writing, as in her life, she revelled in change, disguise, mystery and mimicry....It gave her freedom" (Tomalin 89).

Mansfield's work gives the reader many clues into the workings of her mind and her past. In her writing, her perspectives on past experiences often shift, and her perspectives on the world may shift also; however, the reader is still able to gain insight into Mansfield. This insight helps greatly when attempting to understand her enigmatic personality motives, actions and volatile emotional states. In "Prelude," for example, the reader picks up clues that help in understanding Mansfield's mysterious need to remain mobile. "The women of the family," in "Prelude," "are full of dissatisfactions and dreams of escape" (Tomalin 162). These women, Linda Burnell and Aunt Beryl in particular, are hampered by a vague feeling of dissatisfaction. This feeling occasionally becomes more pronounced than vague, and both Linda and Beryl vent their frustrations in part through fantasies of leaving all of this behind. Beryl, the unmarried aunt, fantasizes about a wonderful young man suddenly arriving to rescue her from a life of loneliness.

Yet, there is something else, too, "something at the back of Beryl's mind, something she did not even put into words for herself" (237). Beryl seems to associate her isolation in the country with death. As she writes to a friend, "But buried, my dear. Buried isn't the word" (259). In the character of Beryl, especially, the reader can learn much about Mansfield herself. Like Beryl, Mansfield seemed to have a constant dissatisfaction with the state of her life. She was, from the beginning, convinced that she was destined for great things, and destined to be a great person. Beryl cries at one point, "I'm always acting a part. I'm never my real self for a moment" (262). Throughout her life, Mansfield also seemed to follow this same kind of pattern of role-playing, and it can be associated very closely with her constant need to move away. Mansfield is always responding to her feeling that she could be more, that she could attain greater things.

Being always in the company of strangers meant KM was never required to be consistent—to be one distinctive self without change—without freedom. She, by continually role-playing, could live outside the ordinary boundaries of identity and explore different lives without ever risking loss of control. Hornby in *Drama, Metadrama, and Perception* discusses role-playing and identity. He suggests "When one remains in the same place, he is certain of encountering, more or less, the same small group of people everyday throughout a lifetime. In such cases one can be fairly comfortable about identity. People do not try to hide who they are because it would do no good when always dealing with the same people. But when one is always dealing with new people trickery becomes imminently possible" (Hornby 78). Katherine played with this idea all her life. She studied deception, used it to create roles and entrance people, and then did exactly as she liked.

Her obsession with masks—roles—is reflected in both her life and her writings. She saw life as a continual state of required self-falsifications. Her perception of existence was founded in "the clash between the self that exists in the world in its masked and in authentic form, and the vulnerable, confused, unstructured self beneath the mask" (Fullbrook 9). She believed that the acceptance of a fixed identity would open the individual to complete oppression and she refused to allow this to happen. She would not acquiesce to such a fixture. She sought for "the removal of limitation from the individual" (Fullbrook 25). For KM, to define meant to confine. To limit oneself to a single, fixed identity was the ultimate crime against the individual self. She wanted a freer existence. She wanted to "Try all sorts of lives—one [was] so very small" (Tomalin 30). In response to Polonius's advice to Hamlet, "to thine own self be true," KM says:

> True to oneself? Which self? Which of my many—well, really, that's what it looks like it's coming to—hundreds of selves? For what with complexes and repressions and reactions and vibrations and reflections, there are moments when I feel I am nothing but the small clerk of some hotel without a proprietor, who has all his work cut out to enter the names and hand the keys to the willful guests. (Fullbrook 18)

When Mansfield returned to London at 20, she was an ambitious, rebellious woman, "confident that an exciting destiny must be awaiting her there" (Tomalin 46). During these young years, Mansfield often used people to get where she wanted to be. She presented herself as a slightly different person to each of these people, and her life was in constant turbulence. She moved from place to place, taking on new identities, each to fit her new situation. In this state of her life, Mansfield was striving to reach her ambitious goals. One of these goals was to lead a life that would not meet with the approval of her parents, to lead a life that was not patterned after the ideals of "Victorian womanhood" (Tomalin 46). She saw herself as a person far beyond that, and many of her wanderings at this point result from her adventures as this new woman.

Mansfield soon met Murry, and their life together can be seen as a new stage in Mansfield's life of moving. Much of her moving after she entered into this relationship was in reaction to the same kind of feeling that both Linda and Beryl feel in "Prelude." As KM moved in and out of her life, she was torn between her need for the security of Murry's reassuring love, and her need for independence to attain the heights that she felt herself capable of both as a writer and as a new, independent woman. The culmination of these emotions was Mansfield's alternating moods of complete dependence on Murry and equally complete resentment of him. Mansfield was seldom satisfied. Every time she and Murry moved to a new cottage, she felt sure that this was a new beginning. However, very soon she would feel the same suffocation. KM describes Linda in much the say way when Linda sees "herself driving away from them all in a little buggy, driving away from everybody and not even waving" (Murry 232). Beryl advises a moth that has flown into the house to "Fly away before it is too late" (Murry 256). This seems to be the feeling that Mansfield continually had.

KM considered the self as multiple, shifting, non-consecutive, without essence, and perhaps unknowable. In her view, the creation of a mask—the consciously wrought presentation of a coherent, yet artificial, self—was required in order for individuals to protect themselves from the constant danger of fragmentation. She wanted desperately to believe in the possibility of a continuous, consistent self that might allow release from prescribed roles and masks; though, while she was attracted to the idea, she could never truly accept it. "It was not that Katherine always wanted to wear a mask; but she felt that if she let it slip down she would perhaps lose herself—her roles..." (Tomalin 180). While one person describes her as guarded—"the pale face is a quiet mask....But she is cautious, a bit suspicious, on her guard" (Tomalin 155)—another might describe her as open, straightforward, accessible. She purposely created these roles, and moving always gave her the freedom to do so.

Mansfield spent her final years as an invalid, dying of tuberculosis. It is intriguing to note that even during this time, Mansfield was usually on the move. She moved to Switzerland, France and Italy in search of the perfect climate or the right treatment that would cure her. The accepted prescribed treatment for tuberculosis victims at this time was for patients to stay wherever they were, and spend time in a nearby sanatorium. Mansfield, however, searched for doctors who would give her different advice. She seemed absolutely incapable of accepting this usual prescription of treatment—life confined to a sanatorium. Her refusal is not very hard to understand when we consider what that treatment would entail, a long, heavily supervised stay in one place. This probably would have killed Mansfield just as quickly as tuberculosis. In 1922, still looking for a cure, Mansfield moved to a commune in Paris and died there in January of 1923.

Katherine Mansfield, in her search for a life free from boundaries and social constraints, used moving as her method of attainment. Knowing the brevity and the limitations of her life, she refused to accept the conditions society attempted to impose upon her. She lived as she chose to live. Her different roles gave her what she perceived as freedom—freedom from the complacent existence that most people settle for. Always moving—always changing roles—prevented her from being confined by other people and their ideas, which is what she fought against her entire life. She eluded everyone. Always moving, always changing, she successfully defied neat definitions and categories, and maintained control in almost every situation.

Sources

Fullbrook, Kate. *Katherine Mansfield*. Sussex: The Harvester Press Limited, 1986.

Hornby, Richard. *Drama, Metadrama, and Perception*. New Jersey: Associated UP, 1986.

Murry, John Middleton. *Katherine Mansfield and Other Literary Studies*. London: Constable, 1959.

Tomalin, Claire. *Katherine Mansfield: A Secret Life*. New York: Alfred A. Knopf, 1988.

Chapter Two
Three Critical Perspectives on Mansfield's Fiction

In her 1980 book *Narratology: Introduction to the Theory of Narrative*, Dutch literary critic Mieke Bal sets out to present a "*systematic* account of a theory of narrative for use in the study of literary and other narrative texts" (ix). Bal has three aims in proposing the theory: to integrate various types of theories, to show the need for rational critical discourse, and to follow the study of narrative as a genre. More specifically she targets her book at readers who view the narrative as she does, as "a mode of cultural self-expression" (ix). The critic defines narratology as the theory of narrative texts, a set of general statements about a corpus, although Bal is quick to admit the difficulty in establishing the boundaries of the corpus or, to put it another way, the difficulty of answering the question, what should be considered a narrative text? The answer may seem obvious—newspaper articles, short stories and novels are narrative texts. Bal points out, though, that in setting up parameters for the corpus one increases the chance of disagreement among researchers, some of whom might argue that a comic strip—say Matt Groening's "Life in Hell"—should be regarded as narrative text.

The inclusion of cartoons stretches the idea of text in Bal's view, for she defines text as "a finite, structured whole composed of language signs" (5). From this definition three others, equally significant, spring.

A *narrative text* is a text in which an agent relates a narrative. A *story* is a fabula that is presented in a certain manner. A *fabula* is a series of logically and chronologically related events that are caused or experienced by actors. (5)

Fabula, story and text. Bal takes the three-layered distinction as the basis for her narrative theory, and in order to understand better narratology, we must examine each layer in more depth. Thus, the

14

following paragraphs will describe an important characteristic of each layer, and will take as illustrations actions, characters, and sentences from Mansfield's story, "The Fly."

Structuralist critics before Bal, most notably Roland Barthes, assume there exists between the sentence and the whole text a homology, a corresponding relationship of position, value, structure, or function. These critics also believe that a similar relationship can be discerned between the "deep structure" of the sentence and that of the narrative text which is the fabula, and believe that understanding the "deep structure" will lead to a more valid interpretation of the text. Although she doesn't dismiss the homology, Bal prefers to see fabulas as being constructed "according to the demands of human 'logic of events'" (12). This logic of events is what we readers perceive and experience in the world. Therefore, "events" are a significant element in the fabula layer of Bal's narratology and are defined as a process, or as "the transition from one state to another state, caused or experienced by actors" (13). As in establishing the corpus of narrative texts, however, determining which sentences are events can be difficult, but Bal offers her three criteria—change, choice and confrontation.

In "The Fly," for example, the boss's killing of the fly meets these criteria and is thus an event. The change, of course, occurs with the fly's death because the insect moves from one state, life, to another, death. The boss's action exhibits choice; he can drop another flood of ink on the fly or not, and that he chooses to drop the ink a second, then a third time determines the outcome of the fabula. Confrontation exists between the human and the insect and may be stated linguistically as a simple sentence: subject—verb—direct object: the boss kills the fly. But one event does not make a fabula, for Bal defines a fabula as a "series of logically and chronologically related events," and it is only through a study of the structure of the series of events that interpretation becomes possible.

In Mansfield's story the series might be expressed as follows: Woodifield visits the boss; he cannot remember what he wishes to say; the boss gives him whiskey; Woodifield remembers what he wishes to say; he tells the boss about the boss's son's grave; the boss remembers his son; the fly distracts him; the boss kills the fly; the boss cannot recall what he was thinking of. The series constitutes a process, and a process to Bal may be either one of improvement or deterioration. Here Mansfield's story confounds easy classification, for if we see the boss's inability to call up his son's memory as proof that time heals all wounds, the process seems one of improvement; but if we interpret the events as evidence that the boss has forgotten his son rather quickly and thus, in spite of his protests, never really cared for the boy, the process shows deterioration. Since the boss's torturing and killing of the fly leads readers to an unsympathetic reading of his character, the process is most likely one of deterioration. We have discussed events in detail here, even though there are other elements of the fabula such as actors, time and location, for Bal considers events as the most relevant component. Events and how they are presented also play an important part in the next level, that of story.

As we saw earlier, the structuralist critic defines story as a "fabula that is presented in a certain manner," so that at this level "ordering" becomes the main consideration. Now the query is not "What is the fabula?" but "How is the fabula ordered and presented to the reader?" To answer the question Bal elaborates on story aspects which include sequential ordering, rhythm, characters, and space, but she sees perspective, or point of view, as the "prime means of manipulation (of the elements of the fabula)" (50). Events are shown from within a "certain vision," and there naturally exists a relation between that which is presented and the vision through which it is presented (100). However, Bal does not use the current labels of point of view or perspective in discussing that relation because she believes that labels are inadequate. They fail, she states, to distinguish "between *those who see* and *those who speak*" (101). In other words, Bal draws a distinction between the vision itself and the voice which verbalizes the vision, and the term she chooses to use is "focalization."

This relationship must be studied in regards to its two parts; that is, the subject and the object of focalization. The subject Bal terms the "focalizor" which she defines as "the point from which the elements are viewed" and which may exist either internally or externally in the story (104). The internal focalizor is a participating character in the fabula through whose eyes and opinions the events are filtered, while the external focalizor is an "anonymous agent" who lies outside the fabula (105). Naturally, a story's having an internal focalizor raises many questions regarding the character's accuracy in reporting and interpreting events, but the same questions also must be asked about an external focalizor who, even though seemingly objective, may be equally biased. An interesting point that Bal makes is that focalization in a story may shift among characters or even alternate between internal and external focalizors. We find this happening in "The Fly" where the external focalizor sometimes relinquishes "the point from which the elements are viewed" to the boss who then shares his vision with readers.

The second part of the relationship is the focalized object. Bal poses questions which must be answered in regards to the object: first, "*what* does the character focalize?" and second, "*how* does it do this?" (106). In KM's story, the boss, viewing the fly as it cleans itself of the ink, presents his vision of the struggling insect to readers. The fly is the boss's focalized object, whereas the attitude he takes toward it—the "how" of Bal's question—changes from admiration ("He's a plucky little devil") to disdain ("Look sharp") to despair ("a grinding feeling of wretchedness seized him"). At the same time, one step back from the fabula, the external focalizor views the boss torturing the fly and offers readers a second, "more objective" vision of the events. That the view of the internal focalizor can only be given through the "all encompassing" vision of the external focalizor leads the critic to conclude "there is no fundamental difference between a 'first-person narrative' and a 'third-person narrative'," a conclusion we will examine more closely as we move into the third level of Bal's narratology (111).

The third and final level of the structuralist's theory deals with narrative text, defined by Bal as "a text in which a narrative agent tells a story" (119). Whereas at the fabula level we concerned ourselves with the events shown and at the story level with the ordering and presentation of those events, at the narrative level we are interested in *who* does the telling. According to the critic, the narrative agent, or narrator, is never a person and certainly never the biographical author of the story, and thus, we cannot claim that Katherine Mansfield is the narrator of "The Fly."

The narrator itself is a creation rather than an extension of the writer and must be studied separately as a function. Terming the narrator "the most central concept in the analysis of narrative texts," Bal notes the close relationship between it and the focalizor which, she suggests, may be related to the idea that our language shapes our vision (120). Bal concludes that "*seeing*, taken in the widest sense, constitutes the object of *narrating*" (121).

Now in "The Fly," the narrator doesn't reveal itself through use of the personal "I" or through asides to "dear reader" and therefore seems invisible; this does not mean, however, that there is no narrator. For Bal argues that with language there must be a speaker and with narrative text, a narrator. Take this example from the story. "The boss lifted the corpse on the end of the paper knife and flung it into the waste-paper basket." The narrator becomes apparent if we rewrite the sentence as follows: "(I say) The boss lifted the corpse on the end of the paper knife and flung it into the waste-paper basket." Since all sentences in a story may be prefaced with "I say" or "I narrate," Bal argues that "the term 'third-person narrator' is absurd" (122). " 'I' " and 'he' are both 'I' (121). But the critic does draw a distinction between the character-bound narrator, a character in the fabula who narrates, and the external narrator, who is not an actor in the fabula. Here the narrative intention differs. The character-bound narrator often seems to be writing autobiography, whereas the external narrator seems to be testifying to the truth of the events it presents. Thus, we can rewrite a sentence from Mansfield's story like this: "[I narrate: (I testify):] Then the front legs waved, took hold, and pulling its small sodden body up it [the fly] began the immense task of cleaning ink from its wings." Going further, Bal also offers a formula by which to express the above interpretation—EN[CF (the boss)—the fly(p)]. Or, translated, an external narrator [EN] testifies that a character-bound focalizor [CF] observes an actor performing a perceptible [p] act. These three roles—narrator, focalizor, and actor—correspond to and illustrate the different levels of Bal's theory of narratology.

It must be evident by now that Mieke Bal devotes much attention in *Narratology: Introduction to the Theory of Narrative* to attempting to classify the components of a narrative text. She sees no way around classification if the ordering principles of her theory are to be made clear, but at the same time, she states that classification in itself is not an end but a means in literary scholarship, meaningful only as far as it helps to describe text. This is her goal—to provide a theory which will make possible a complete description that accounts for the narrative characteristics of a text. Such a description will serve as a foundation for interpretation. Bal writes that "it is possible on the basis of description ('the text is so constructed') to attach a meaning to the text ('the text means this')" (9-10). This is what the structuralist's theory is intended to do. What her theory is not intended to do is act as a "kind of machine into which one inserts a text at one end and expects an adequate description to roll out at the other" (3). Regardless of a reader's point of departure—and with Bal it is feminist criticism—theory, any literary theory, should only be considered a useful tool for interpreting a narrative, and never should a theory overshadow the work itself. We read Mieke Bal to understand better a Katherine Mansfield story, but we read Mansfield, first and last, to understand better human experience.

In his chapter "Stylistics and the Teaching of Literature" in *Languages and Literature*, M.H. Short points out that though basically alike in written prose, there is an important difference between the presentation of speech and thought. The norm for the presentation of speech is direct speech (DS), whereas for the presentation of thought the norm is indirect thought (IT) "because it is semantically implausible to suggest that we can directly observe the thoughts of others" (Short 184).

			norm ↓		
Speech Presentation:	NRSA	IS	FIS	DS	FDS
Thought Presentation:	NRTA	IT	FIT	DT	FDT
	↑ norm				

The difference is important because it explains the difference in effect obtained when the Free Indirect category is used for speech and thought. Because FIT, in opposition to FIS, is a movement from the norm towards the character end of the continuum, it is perceived by readers as representing closeness with that character, the direct observation of the articulation of his thoughts. (Short 184)

"Something Childish but Very Natural," written in December 1912, is among those stories which mark a drastic change in KM's method of fiction. Her works to that point, collected in *In a German Pension* (1911), are told in the I-form; Mansfield assumes the role of the leading character and tells the story entirely from that perspective. *In a German Pension* represents a "youthful immature phase in Katherine's authorship" (Friis 25), and Mansfield eventually disowned her first stories completely, calling them juvenile, and refused to allow them to be reprinted despite the financial security their publications would have meant to her. In her subsequent stories, however, there is a notable change in her narrative method. She drops the I-form and "withdraws more and more behind the work" (Friis 123):

She eliminates everything which may remind the reader of the writer's personality. All description is rendered as the impression of one of the characters, or in the form of direct speech; descriptive passages which cannot be transformed into such impressions are abolished. (Friis 124)

In "Something Childish but Very Natural" we can see Mansfield moving to that stage; she is in the process of redefining her style. The stories employing this change in narrative form mark a significant change in Mansfield's writing career.

According to John Middleton Murry, "Something Childish but Very Natural" is the result of Mansfield's dealing with the conflict between "Love and Disillusion; Disillusion and Love" and is "saturated with wistful and childlike idealism" (Murry 75). This conflict is eventually resolved by Mansfield and changes into her philosophy of affirming beauty while remaining aware of "the snail under the leaf" (Daly 23). The awareness of the cruel realities of life is a theme in "Something Childish but Very Natural" and many other KM stories.

"Something Childish but Very Natural" is the story of Henry and Edna, two teenagers who meet on an afternoon train and begin an immediate and intense romance. The young lovers go to concerts together, send letters to one another, and daydream about a life without care and responsibility, a life where money and age are inconsequential. In the final scene of the story, Henry is in the cottage they have decided to rent together waiting impatiently for

Edna's arrival. Their renting the cottage is an obvious attempt to make their dream a reality; however, Edna never arrives, only a telegram does. Henry opens it but does not move. The story ends.

Though the relationship between Henry and Edna is intense and their love seems real to them, the superficiality of their intimacy is revealed by the resolution of the plot, and, more subtly, by Mansfield's manner of thought presentation. Throughout the story, Henry's thoughts and feelings are revealed in each of the possible methods of thought presentation; however, at no point are *Edna's* thoughts disclosed. This one-sidedness of their relationship becomes manifestly clear when Edna does not come to the cottage. The reality of her lack of intimacy is demonstrated stylistically.

From the very beginning, the story is told from Henry's perspective, the first sentence being the narrative report of a thought act (NRTA):

Whether he had forgotten what it felt like, or his head had really grown bigger since the summer before, Henry could not decide. But his straw hat hurt him... (164)

Mixed with the pure narrative of the story are the thoughts of Henry presented as free indirect thought (FIT), direct thought (DT), and free direct thought (FDT). For example, as Henry waits for his train to depart, he glances through an anthology of English poetry and encounters "Something Childish but Very Natural." His delight with the poem is expressed in FIT:

He could not have done with the little poem. It was not the words so much as the whole air of it that charmed him. He might have written it lying in bed, very early in the morning, and watching the sun dance on the ceiling. (165-166)

After he meets Edna and they have exchanged their first words, Henry's exhilaration is again expressed in FIT:

Why on earth should those words have made Henry feel so free suddenly and so happy and so madly excited? What was happening between them? They said nothing, but to Henry their silence was alive and warm. It covered him from his head to his feet in a trembling wave. Her marvelous words, 'It's made a mark,' had in some mysterious fashion established a bond between them. They could not be utter strangers to each other if she spoke so simply and so naturally. And now she was really smiling. The smile danced in her eyes, crept over her cheeks to her lips and stayed there. He leant back. The words flew from him.—'Isn't life wonderful!' (168)

The first part of this paragraph is clearly Henry's thoughts revealed in free indirect style (even though the use of the third-person pronoun is not constant), from the two questions at least down to the sixth sentence. The sixth sentence, "They could not be utter strangers to each other..." is obviously Henry's rationalization of what has transpired between him and Edna. The rest of the paragraph can be read as straight narrative though it is marked by Henry's romantic tone, i.e., "the smile danced," "The words flew."

In addition to frequent sections of FIT, the first part of the story (to the point where the relationship begins) contains several instances of Henry's direct and free direct thoughts:

"She must think I'm mad," he thought, "dashing into a train without even a hat, and in the evening, too." (166)

"I suppose she goes to some school in London," thought Henry. "She might be in an office. Oh, no, she is too young. Besides she'd have her hair up if she was. It isn't even down her back." He could not keep his eyes off that beautiful waving hair. " 'My eyes are like two drunken bees...' Now, I wonder if I read that or made it up?" (166)

"How beautiful she is! How simply beautiful she is!" sang Henry's heart....(167)

"I shall have to speak—have to—have to!" (167)

Eventually Henry and Edna meet on the evening train for a second time. They exchange names and begin their mutual feelings of affection. At this point, the direct and free direct thoughts of Henry cease. The account of their feelings and their activities is related in straight narrative and direct and free direct speech. And even though Edna is now playing a major role in the story, we still do not gain access to her private thoughts.

Two passages of FIT give the initial impression of belonging to Edna; however, closer examination shows they are actually the thoughts of Henry. For example, as they wait for the concert to begin, Henry offers to hold the program for Edna and to read it to her. She rejects him both times. Henry whispers her name, and she pleads, "Oh, please don't. Not here—the people." A lengthy paragraph of free indirect thought follows:

Why did he want to touch her so much and why did she mind? Whenever he was with her he wanted to hold her hand or take her arm when they walked together, or lean against her—not hard—just lean lightly so that his shoulder should touch her shoulder—and she wouldn't even have that. All the time that he was away from her he was hungry, he craved the nearness of her. There seemed to be comfort and warmth breathing from Edna that he needed to keep him calm. Yes, that was it. He couldn't get calm with her because she wouldn't let him touch her. But she loved him. He knew that. Why did she feel so curiously about it? Every time he tried to or even asked for her hand she shrank back and looked at him with pleading frightened eyes as though he wanted to hurt her. They could say anything to each other. And there wasn't any question of their belonging to each other. And yet he couldn't touch her. Why, he couldn't even help her off with her coat. Her voice dropped into his thoughts. (173)

The fact that these are Henry's thoughts is verified by the last sentence in the paragraph and by the content as well; however, the first two sentences, on first reading, could be perceived as Edna's feelings. Because it is immediately preceded by Edna's plea, the first question, "Why did he want to touch her so much and why did she mind?" could easily be read as her expression of frustration. The second sentence conveys much the same feeling. The third sentence, on the other hand, contains sentiments that could not be Edna's. Only Henry could say that he "craved the nearness of her." The fourth sentence of the paragraph lexically confirms the passage as Henry's FIT when Edna's name is substituted for the third person pronoun "she." As "he" is used instead of "Henry," it is clear that Henry's thoughts are being portrayed here.

Another deceptive passage of FIT occurs during the young lovers' second meeting on the train as they trade pertinent information about ages, jobs, and families.

"Isn't it hot?" she said suddenly, and pulled off her grey gloves and put her hands to her cheeks and kept them there. Their eyes were not frightened—they looked at each other with a sort of desperate calmness. If only their bodies would not tremble so stupidly! Still half hidden by her hair, Edna said:

"Have you ever been in love before?" (170)

The sentence of FIT, "If only their bodies would not tremble so stupidly!" is positioned amid straight narrative which is both immediately preceded and followed by speeches of Edna's. The location of the FIT in this case could possibly lead to the conclusion that the thought is Edna's; however, the substance of the passage indicates that it could easily be Henry's. Obvious confusion is created by the location of this brief passage of FIT; nevertheless, it is unlikely that Mansfield would allow Edna only one sentence of FIT in the story. Therefore, since it is from Henry's perspective that all other free indirect thoughts are reported, this passage probably is Henry's as well.

Because Mansfield devotes all the thought passages in this story to Henry, she forces readers to consider "Something Childish but Very Natural" from a different vantage point. After analyzing the story stylistically, one begins to see it as the story of Henry rather than the story of Henry and Edna. The fact that only Henry is allowed every section of thought presentation established his dominance. At the same time, Edna's lacking thought presentation technically parallels her hesitation to give herself over completely, her resistance to intimacy. Edna's actions confirm her desire to stay at arm's length from Henry both literally and figuratively. She does not want Henry to touch her:

Somehow I feel if once we did that—you know—held each other's hands and kissed it would all be changed—and I feel we wouldn't be free like we are— we'd be doing something secret.... I'd feel awkward with you, Henry, and I'd feel shy, and I do so feel that just because you and I are you and I, we don't need that sort of thing. (174-175)

In the final scene of the story, Edna's failure to meet Henry at the cottage also exemplifies her reluctance to commit herself to the relationship.

Mansfield's stylistic technique in this story causes the audience to grant their sympathy to Henry. Because we learn virtually all of Henry's innermost feelings and none of Edna's, we tend to identify with Henry. We experience the love affair with Edna as Henry does; and, therefore, we appreciate his pain, understand his disappointment, and learn from his suffering. Through Edna, Henry learns about the cold realities of life. We realize that his fantasy of a life without care and responsibility can never actually exist; it will remain his daydream. It is Edna who will not let Henry forget about practicality:

"What I feel certain of is," said Henry, "That we ought to be living there, now. We oughtn't to wait for things. What's age? You're as old as you'll ever be and so am I. You know," he said, "I have a feeling often that it's dangerous to wait for things—that if you wait for things they only go further and further away."

"But Henry,—money! You see we haven't any money." (177)

"If only we weren't so young..." she said miserably. (ellipses Mansfield's, 178)

As Edna continues to remind Henry that age and money are issues that must be considered, she becomes the "snail under his leaf." The beauty of Henry's dream is invalidated by actualities that Edna brings to light.

Mansfield's theme in "Something Childish but Very Natural" is made clear by the course of events in the story, but a stylistic examination of thought presentation makes doubly apparent Mansfield's point. Because the character of Edna is not given any presentation of thought, readers are directed to Henry as the only method of perception in the story. As a result, we learn the lesson Henry learns. Mansfield deliberately manipulates her options of thought presentation in order to elicit a specific response from her audience, a response that understands and appreciates the distinction between realism and idealism.

In *Story and Discourse*, Seymour Chatman briefly uses Mansfield's "Two Tuppenny Ones, Please" as an example of a non-narrated story. He refers to the unusual story as a dramatic monologue with a twist; whereas most dramatic monologues do not include the comments of a speaker's listener, this story's "interlocutor" has a "simulacrum of voice through dots of ellipsis" which reveal only the listener's intonation (175). Thus the story's mode lies somewhere between monologue and dialogue, as the reader may catch hints of the unheard party's manner in a two-way conversation, but nothing of its feelings. The reader must learn everything from the speaker whose words are presented, since there is no narrator or mediator offering even the slightest description. While Chatman does not apply the term "non-narrated" explicitly to the story, the story is "non-narrated" in the strictest sense, with no "features" to give a sense of third-party presence (196).

But beyond Chatman's brief explanation of the story, one confronts another peculiar problem of narrative form. To apply Chatman's terminology, Mansfield has endowed this "direct presentation" (146) with a strong "implied author" (148), a strong sense of guiding value or opinion. Thus, the narrator may not be totally "absent" as in most non-narrated stories, but may lurk in the background only as a mental presence, overhearing the conversation as does the reader, and filtering or interpreting what it hears according to its cultural and social value system.

While Chatman asserts that all stories do not automatically entail narrators, he acknowledges that all stories are "mediated," since someone composes them. The author is the ultimate mediator, conveying a specific meaning through specific stylistic choices. However, Chatman distinguishes this mediator as the story's designer from the narrator as one of the choices the mediator makes. The "narrator," states Chatman, "is a demonstrable, recognizable entity imminent to the narrative itself"; it is not the author, but a "presence" formed within the narrative to recount the action, setting, and characters to the audience, "no matter how minimally evoked his voice" (33). The narrator may be either "covert," a "voice speaking" without participating in the plot (197), or "overt," an actual character such as the husband in Mansfield's "A Married Man's Story" (33). If no features reveal such a presence, the story is non-narrated.

As a non-narrated story, "Two Tuppenny Ones, Please" has a "direct" form of presentation; like a play, it is a dramatic monologue-dialogue (Chatman implies this ambiguity), the least obviously narrated of any literary mode (146). If one calls it a dialogue, its "speakers" are a woman whom the reader "overhears" and a "friend" who remains faceless, "as if she (as the story's text implies) turned away from us and we could only catch the interrogative intonation at the end of her utterances" (175). Yet this dialogue must have significance to the mediator, and its meaning to the reader depends on an implied importance to the mediator. To the reader, it seems that someone has overheard the conversation and recorded it, attaching certain associations to the words. The reader's inferences from the conversation are the same as the mediator's; thus, the mediator has manipulated the reader.

The mediator has so obviously used the dialogue as a medium for opinion that one senses that the mediator is on the train with the two women; through inference, the reader senses the presence of a third party. Chatman calls such a third party the "implied author;" this is a "principle," states Chatman, "reconstructed by the reader from the narrative." Chatman continues; "(it) is not the narrator, but rather the principle that invented the narrator, along with everything else in the narrative." Since it is not a narrator and has no appearance, it "can *tell* us nothing...it has no voice, no direct means of communicating." Moreover, this implied author "establishes the norms of the narrative," based on "general cultural codes" which have particular relevance at a given place and time (148-49).

Mansfield intrigues the reader with an unusual approach to the implied author. But a narrator seems just as strongly implied. Perhaps the train ride is Mansfield's own experience, and the cultural norms established are so unmistakably Mansfield's that the reader identifies the implied author as Mansfield or as a person with concerns like hers. As Chatman points out, one participant in the conversation remains faceless and unheard; but her facelessness gives the reader a sense of perspective, an angle of view that approaches a setting. So, while no narrator offers description, and the form of discourse is the most direct and minimally descriptive possible, there is a specific point on that train where the reader sits and overhears; this is the point where the implied author sits, and only through that entity in that place can the reader know anything.

Chapter Three
Stories from *In a German Pension*

As is the case with most any artist, the need for recognition and acceptance is a very strong motivating factor. In the case of Katherine Mansfield, this need for recognition and acceptance, coupled with her trying to prove her artistic merit to an overbearing and hypocritical father, was the primary factor in her publishing her first volume of collected short stories, *In a German Pension*. *In a German Pension* was published in London by Stephen Swift in 1911, and in this first volume, her stories, for the most part, reflect the progressive maturity of an artist. Since it is her first volume, the Mansfield we have is an unformed, struggling writer who is both trying to achieve notoriety and prove to her father that this rebellion from her father was necessary in her development as an artist. When the volume was published, it received rave reviews, and KM had partially accomplished her purpose. "Thus at long last Kathleen was vindicated in front of the whole family" (Alpers 145).

But the contents of this volume reflect the artistic immaturity of the writer. That "the majority of the stories of *In a German Pension* are told in the I form" (Friis 121) is rather significant. Mansfield had not yet mastered the technique of going into a principle character's psyche to determine the inter-workings therein. Also, the experiences she relates are largely autobiographical. "In the sketches of *In a German Pension* Katherine Mansfield is herself the teller of the stories, which are made up by her experience during her stay as a convalescent at Woerishofen in Bavaria in 1909" (Friis). The critics' response to *In a German Pension* was largely positive, but in comparing these stories to the later Mansfield, "the stories of *In a German Pension* represent a phase of cynicism and disillusionment; the world is amusing, but rather despicable; people in it are ridiculous and rather stupid" (Friis 168). The major limitations of this volume are

28

significant. That most of the stories are written in the first person about life experiences shows that KM had not, at this point in her career, been able to transcend her own experience and distance herself from her art (to whatever degree that is possible). Even Mansfield realized the limitations of this volume. In 1920, KM forbade republication of this volume under any circumstances. Alpers notes that "(*In a German Pension*) was 'positively juvenile'—it wasn't what she meant—it was a lie" (Alpers 288). However, KM began to progress both emotionally and artistically, and this increasing maturity is evidenced in her next volume. But by the same token, for all its amateurities and immaturity, *In a German Pension* also has stories that breathe fire and truly powerful feelings.

KM's writing style began to change in 1911. This was the time that she met John Middleton Murry, and she was also going through an unsettled period in her life. In 1908, she had an affair with Garnet Trowell; in 1909 she was married to George Bowden for one day; also in 1909 she gave birth to a stillborn child. It was out of these circumstances that Mansfield wrote *In a German Pension*. During the wretched years of her convalescence, Mansfield wrote the somewhat bitter, cynical, and satirical stories included in this volume. "These stories emphasize her role as outsider in a hostile world" (Meyers 50). "At Lehmann's" and "A Birthday" concern the difficulty of childbirth. Even though Mansfield often wrote and dreamed about having a child, she never had one.

"Germans at Meat"

As one of Mansfield's satirical pieces on Germany, "Germans at Meat" offers a harsh two-fold display of German chauvinism: on one hand, as the English narrator sits down for food and conversation with Germans, she finds herself amid chauvinistic males proud of their virility and eager for their wives to bear children; on the other hand, the Germans measure the viability of neighbor societies by dietary habits. Thus, two levels of metaphor work through the same vehicle: food. Mansfield's statement is at once an indictment of sexism and an examination of the social and political tensions of Europe before the first world war.

The narrator is an English woman visiting Bavaria for a

"cure," presumably a vacation prescribed by her doctor. Thus any confrontation with German natives may expose her to the chauvinism and force her to defend her homeland or to retreat to it. She would rather avoid the bold verbal jousts the Germans launch at her, and she remains civil throughout the scene in an attempt to maintain diplomacy; however, she is an obvious target for ridicule. The Germans condescend to her for two reasons. First, she does not fulfill the criteria for German womanhood. When a German woman asks her what meat her husband likes most, she replies that she does not know; moreover, she is a vegetarian, and to Germans a vegetarian woman could not possibly find the strength to bear a suitable number of children. Thus, she cannot "expect to keep her husband" satisfied. Second, her shortcomings and undesirability as a woman are extended into a larger social and political significance. The Germans believe they are superior militarily and culturally to the British, and that they could easily overwhelm the British: "We don't want England," proclaims one German; "If we did we would have had her long ago" (38). To the Germans the narrator must seem as weak as her nation's army—"a few little boys with their veins full of nicotine poisoning" (40). The Germans find evidence of her weakness when she refuses the sauerkraut as "a little strong," as well as in the "preposterous" English breakfast for which they expect her to account. English tea-making techniques seem petty to the Germans, especially when the narrator admits that tea is "one thing" she does well, a tacit admission of feminine inadequacy for herself and for Britain. Moreover, a German male's ability to cook is a sign of masculinity, and that masculine ability must extend beyond merely making good tea.

The narrator thus faces a conflict between supposedly masculine and feminine societies; but that conflict is more precisely sexual. The voracious German appetite for sauerkraut, bread, soup, and beef contrasts sharply with the narrator's vegetarian diet; the more gluttonous the diet, the more virile the man, and the more willing the woman is to cater to this gluttony, the more worthy she is sexually. The conflict arises from the male insistence on predominance: as the Germans insist on dominating all of Europe culturally and politically, so most males dominate women sexually and so must women submit. The Germans impose a sense of inadequacy on the narrator when she refuses to submit to masculine will—like the English "suffragettes" to which a submissive German woman contemptuously refers. Indeed, the overbearing masculinity frightens the narrator, and in the end, she leaves the room as the Germans demand more food—*"Mahlzeit!"* As they demand their meal, they demand sex.

"The Baron"

"The Baron" opens with the narrator, an English woman, eating with German acquaintances. She notices a man eating alone and asks who he is. A German woman replies with disgust at such ignorance, that he is a Baron. During the following weeks, the narrator is captivated by the mysteriousness of the Baron. On the rainy day before his departure, the Baron asks the narrator if she would like to share his umbrella as they walk to the boarding house. After this conversation, she is treated quite differently by the other women.

Hostility is a dominant theme in this Mansfield story. The postman represents the German hostility as he throws the narrator's mail into her milk pudding. The Baron displays his lack of trust in people by carrying his black bag close to him everywhere he goes. The rain acts as a symbol of the world's hostility which is actually what brought the two together in the end.

Isolation also brought the narrator to the Baron. She was alienated from the German women because of her ignorance of their culture. The Baron was also isolated from the whole community because of both his position in society as well as by his choice to be alone and therefore uncontaminated. In the end they find each other and share a meeting full of understanding.

"Frau Brechenmacher Attends a Wedding"

Mansfield's "Frau Brechenmacher Attends a Wedding" is a story about a woman named Frau Brechenmacher and her husband, Herr Brechenmacher, who are completely swamped by the daily routines of life until the day they attend the wedding of "Fancy Theresa," a woman who is ridiculed by her community for not only having a child illegitimately, but also for bringing it to the wedding (1). The Frau, who finds her greatest satisfaction in the privacy of her home, finds it difficult adjusting to the kinds of social interactions that take place at such a wedding. Therefore, the entire evening turns into an evening of shame when the Frau convinces herself that her inability to adjust has become the focal point of the evening.

Frau Brechenmacher, the central figure in the story, enjoys nurturing her five babies and taking care of her husband. Her normal day begins with feeding her children, ironing Herr's postman's uniform, making sure all of his buttons are in place, dressing in the dark while Herr dresses in the light, then sending her husband out the door with a kiss. Her life is so routine that when there are any deviations from the normal, the Frau feels threatened and unappreciated. On the one hand, the Frau feels threatened by her daughter, Rosa, who is capable of taking care of her siblings as well as the Frau. On the other hand, the Frau feels unappreciated by society because despite the fact that she is a hard-working, loyal, dedicated wife, she does not receive the kind of recognition a woman should who has five children and is married to a prestigious man.

The conflict arises in the story when the Frau and Herr Brechenmacher attend "Fancy Theresa's" wedding. Herr experiences no difficulty when it comes to socializing; therefore, he helps himself to the abundance of alcoholic beverages that surround him, and in the process, he becomes intoxicated. Quite the contrary, Frau Brechenmacher is not accustomed to all the drinking and dancing that occur at a wedding. She plans a quiet entrance to the wedding, only to find that all eyes are on her because she has forgotten to close the back of her skirt. After she gets over her embarrassment, she begins enjoying the ceremony and reminiscing about her childhood. When the Frau realizes that no one is going to ask her to dance, she becomes cognizant that this is not the caliber of people with whom she feels the most comfortable.

Hence, when Herr makes his presentation to the couple, everyone finds humor in his speech except the Frau. While staring around the room, she concludes that all the people are laughing at her more than her husband's speech. What are they laughing at? According to the Frau, they are laughing at her not only because she is somewhat of a "misfit," but also because it seems that the other women are stronger than she and possess something she does not—the ability to have a good time. After the evening has ended, the Frau does not feel as though she is in her rightful capacity until she returns home, takes care of her babies, and feeds her husband. This is what makes Frau the happiest, and in turn, she does not have to deal with the social pressures of life.

"The Modern Soul"

"The Modern Soul" opens with the female narrator sitting with Herr Professor while he graces her with his conversation and far superior knowledge. The two Godowska women approach, and after a brief conversation, all four return to the pension for the evening recital in which Sonia and the Professor perform separate acts. Sonia invites the narrator to an evening walk which abruptly ends as Sonia dramatically faints outside the hairdresser's shop. Naturally, the Professor runs to her aid. The next morning the female narrator learns at breakfast that the Professor and Sonia are spending the day in the woods.

There is a sharp contrast between appearance and reality in this story. The Professor and Sonia are the world of appearance. The Professor requests that the narrator not leave when the Godowskas approach because he is afraid of how the situation might appear to the two women. His confrontation with reality is that he must pay for his late-night milk. In comparison, Sonia spends her whole life pretending to be what she is not with a career of acting. Her tragedy or conflict with reality is her mother who so thoughtfully points out a visible safety pin in her skirt. Although Sonia is labeled a "modern soul" by the Professor, it is the Professor who acts as the real "sole" upon which Sonia walks all over through her grand performance. Mansfield's narrator sees straight through Sonia as the narrator leaves Sonia having fainted outside the hairdresser's window, knowing Sonia was in no real danger. The narrator also notes that "modern souls oughtn't to wear (stays)" (81). This also strengthens the point that Sonia tries to *appear* to be a modern soul, but in actuality is not.

The story is filled with sexual images and allusions. The Professor proudly stating the fact that he has eaten such a quantity of fruit can be seen as notches on his belt counting the number of women he has had the pleasure of enjoying. Sonia adorns herself with flowers which represent Spring and the season of fertility. Even in her performance she extends a sensuous invitation of going into the woods "as lightly draped as possible, and bed among the pine needles" (68). Another obvious allusion to promiscuity is that fact that the Professor must "loosen her stays" which he willingly does or so the reader assumes. The Professor, at the beginning of the story, had emerged from the woods only to return to nature, at the end of the story, for enjoyment with Sonia.

"At Lehmann's"

At first reading, the plot of "At Lehmann's" is rather complex; however, after careful study, one sees that this is clearly a story revealing the sexual awakening of an innocent, overworked young girl—Sabina. Sabina is employed by Herr and Frau Lehmann as a waitress in their cafe/restaurant. She also assists in caring for Frau Lehmann, who is pregnant. Although Frau Lehmann is described as being "a big woman at the best of time" (73) she has grown enormously large during her pregnancy; at her husband's request she is confined to her quarters, for she "looked unappetising" (73). Sabina resides in the boardinghouse where she shares a room with the cook, Anna. Because of Sabina's youth and naiveté, Anna takes unwarranted advantage of their working relationship. Sabina must rise early to complete her chores and many of Anna's chores, too, before Herr Lehmann opens the cafe for guests each morning. Hans, the scullery boy, completes the employee team at Lehmann's cafe.

As Sabina scurries from table to table, the women customers inquire about the Frau's health. Although Sabina answers in a confident manner, she is annoyed at her own ignorance because she really does not understand the nature of pregnancy. She readily admits to herself that she understands death; birth is more complicated. What she does not know or understand is "what had the man…to do with it?" (74). As Sabina contemplates the idea of birth, she meets a new and interesting customer, the Young Man. There is something special about his presence; Sabina feels "…Half pleasure, half pain…" He excites her interest in her hair and her body. He even shows her a picture of a naked woman. As Sabina prepares for bed, she thinks for the first time about twisting her "hair back so tightly"; she even wishes for a mirror to examine her small body, for the picture of the naked woman stirs her imagination and arouses her own sexual curiosity.

Although Sabina is really desirous of the Young Man, she is repelled at the same time, for she does not ever want to look like Frau Lehmann or become "unappetising" as the Frau is to Herr Lehmann. Sabina cannot clearly articulate her feelings; however, it is clear that she is making some kind of connection about male/female relationships. The Young Man calls a second time. And, again, his presence exudes warmth. At this meeting, he touches Sabina's hands and breasts and kisses her. When she finally begins to feel like a woman and allows her sexuality to unfold, she is frightened and rushes out, thereby making herself inaccessible. The cry from the Frau's new baby causes Sabina's feelings to change drastically. Somehow, at this point, the connection is clear. She knows the role of the male, and she finds it to be dangerous and repugnant. Her innocent, child-like quality is reflected in her resistance.

Sabina gets faced with a difficult choice. Her struggle is internal. The sexual awakening in this innocent girl is gradually made clear as the story unfolds. At first, she is innocently curious; later she becomes obsessed with her own curiosity. Sabina observes the Frau's fat, swollen and ugly body; she listens to Anna and her friends expound on the Frau's pregnancy; she observes Anna and Hans as they sit and listen to every groan during the Frau's delivery. She, too, hears the strange and awful sounds coming from the Frau's quarters as she labors to give birth. Sabina is confused and agitated with the whole environment. While the Young Man arouses Sabina's feminine instincts, somehow she is not capable of separating her feelings for this man from her feelings about the Frau's dilemma, being pregnant, and finally giving birth. As she breaks the embrace with the Young Man and dashes from the room, it is clear, finally, that she finds all this repulsive, and even, in the end, rejects her sexual awakening.

"The Luft Bad"

As one of Mansfield's satirical dialogues based on her experiences at a Bavarian spa, "The Luft Bad" presents a character surrounded by self-conscious women pre-occupied with trivial matters. As the narrator describes each woman in turn, they form a social "circle" based on strict conformity to glamorous, feminine pursuits—with men looming in the story's background and indirectly influencing the women's attitudes. Because of their conformity, the women seem to exist collectively, with muted individual identities. Yet while the women remain unchanged and absorbed in their "circle," the young, female narrator moves outside the setting of vanity and assumes a defiant posture. Thus, while the women around her seem to have ceased thinking for themselves, the narrator becomes more aware of herself and resolves not to fall into the vanity of her companions.

Mansfield presents the narrator's transition through the image of umbrellas that the women carry as they strut around the spa "very nearly in their nakeds" (79). When the story begins, the narrator is apprehensive about the umbrellas, which create "a distinctly Little Black Sambo touch" (79). As her description suggests, the women are holding symbols of obedience, fulfilling roles of subservience to their social "circle" as well as practicing to satisfy the sexual desires of their men. Clearly the narrator does not accept the role and does not regard herself as a member of the group. As in "Germans at Meat," she is a shy foreigner who feels inept at the customs she encounters. While the other foreigners in the group characterize themselves by trivially self-aggrandizing traits—the Hungarian by her husband's tomb, and the Russian by her whirling "Salome" dance—the narrator offers nothing to distinguish herself within the group. She remains an observer, noting with irreverence the contrast between the lethargic habits of the women and the masculine work of the men.

Yet unlike the diners in "Germans at Meat," the women in the spa are not hostile to the narrator initially; they are perhaps too preoccupied with their habits. Eventually, however, one of the women shows some curiosity about the narrator and asks if she is American or British—"You must be one of the two. You cannot help it" (81). Here, as the narrator leaves the circle of women and climbs onto a swing, she reveals that she considers herself neither British nor American. Contradicting the "vegetable woman," she implies that no one can ascribe a social role to her. The swing works with the umbrella as a central metaphor in the sketch. After the narrator climbs onto the swing, the women reveal their own fears of leaving their roles and feeling, as does the narrator, "free and happy—so childish." Such self-actualizing "is very upsetting" to a hollow identity.

While the narrator returns to the spa when the story ends, she has found a use for the previously silly umbrellas: she hides from other women. But while she is shy about exposing her legs at the beginning, she is proud of them as her own at the end, and she is comfortable away from the "circle." Ironically, conforming to the group proves unnecessary, as the large umbrella is her husband's.

"A Birthday"

A satirical picture of the event of childbirth from a father's point of view, Mansfield's "A Birthday" portrays the roles of men and women, especially within marriage, in a patriarchal culture. Mansfield creates the character of what could be considered the "typical" male, a selfish, self-centered business man with a quite fragile ego. Through the portrayal of his self-centered, petty thoughts and actions, Mansfield attacks the institution of marriage, patriarchal society, and the repressive role of women in that society.

The main character is Andreas Binzer, the expectant father. A character who seems to portray many of the characteristics of Mansfield's father and other men from her childhood, Binzer is Mansfield's vehicle for showing the chauvinistic attitude of men. Binzer goes through this day with thoughts only of himself, while his wife, never seen, only heard, is upstairs going through the agony of childbirth. He is incredibly self-absorbed; taking personally anything anyone says or does; he can only relate the events of the day to himself and how it will affect him. We never once even see him consider going up to check on his wife. It has been left to his *mother*, who has had to stay up the whole night with the wife, to take care of that "frightful business." Binzer sees himself as "sensitive," and views others as taking advantage of this fact. His attitude about his role in the marriage is warped, and through his thoughts concerning his views of things such as the upkeep of the house, the treatment of the children, his rights as a husband and father, Mansfield creates a grim picture of just how hellish the wife's life must be.

The major characteristic of marriage in a patriarchal society is spelled out: the women do all the work, but the men have the

illusion that *they* do. The wife endures the hardships; she always
has something to do. Binzer's wife, for instance, has had "three
children in four years thrown in with the dusting, so to speak"
(88). Of this childbirth, Binzer imagines that he knows "what
suffering is," while he never even witnesses first hand the hell his
wife endures. The wife is always expected to be interested in her
husband and there to fulfill his every need. Binzer notices the
change marriage has brought to his wife, but he never stops to
consider the causes of these changes, or why he, too, has *not*
changed. In addition, Binzer seems to view this change as a fault
of his wife when he states, "Marriage certainly changed a woman
far more than it did a man," because a few sentences later, he
states, "She'd got into a groove; he'd have to force her out of it,
that's all" (90). Binzer seems to look at every problem from the
point of view that it is something for him to take care of, when, in
actuality, his wife is always left with that task. Binzer's
chauvinism is also, of course, displayed in his hoping for a boy to
carry on the family name. It surely would benefit the wife to have
a boy, also, since that is probably the only way she will be able to
stop having children.

The conflict in the story, therefore, exists on two levels. The
conflict on the surface concerns the tensions and anxiety
associated with childbirth. On a thematic level, the conflict
concerns the chauvinistic, self-absorbed attitude of men and the
ensuing repressive roles of women, particularly in marriage. The
surface conflict is resolved in the end with the successful birth of a
healthy baby boy. However, the deeper conflict persists for both
the reader and for Mansfield, who seems to be speaking directly
through the servant girl when she, "in full loathing of mankind,"
vows "herself to sterility" (87).

"The Child-Who-Was-Tired"

"The Child-Who-Was-Tired" is an ironic story about a small
child who is the sole servant to a brutish German family. The irony
lies in the fact that this small girl is expected to forget her
childhood to be a "Mother" to this household. She sets the
Master's breakfast in the morning, packs the children off to
school, minds the baby all day, helps prepare the meals, and does
household chores. The child is deprived of sleep at night because

she is supposed to keep the baby from wetting the bed. The crisis in the story comes when the Master announces that his wife is going to have another baby. The Child is horrified. She is already at the point of exhaustion with her present duties, and the thought of more work haunts her throughout the day. Finally, at the close of that long day, the Child is sent into the bedroom to keep the baby quiet. All she can think of is her desperate longing for sleep, and the appalling notion that another baby is on the way. In an ironic twist, the child hits upon a plan to put the baby permanently to sleep, so "You'll not cry any more or wake up in the night" (99). Only then can she sleep, relieved of her duties.

The small girl in "The Child-Who-Was-Tired" has been taken away from her mother, a "waitress at the railway station" because her mother tried to squeeze her head into a jug. The Child, ironically called "free-born" by the Frau, is thought to be slow-witted. "She looks like an owl. Such children are seldom right in their heads," is the comment from one of the Frau's friends (98). Actually, the Child is a very bright girl who handles the amount of work she is given well, until she is worn down by the lack of sleep and the thought of a new baby coming into the house. But it is more convenient for the Frau to believe her to be stupid and to treat the Child as somewhat less than human. "What do you mean by sleeping like this the whole night through—like a sack of potatoes?" (92). The Child cannot remember her mother, but she remembers a story that someone—probably her mother—told her about a little girl who played all day in the meadow, had sausages and beer for her dinner, and was not tired. Her only memory is thus a good one, and it relates to the childhood the Frau has taken away from her. A telling detail in the story is that the little girl in the story is not tired. Everything in her pitiful life mocks her tiredness. The stove will not light in the morning and "Perhaps it was cold, like herself, and sleepy" (92). The grass the child sees in the meadow would be a wonderful place to sleep, as would the beds she must make up but cannot sleep on.

Because this Child was born a bastard to a mother who apparently did not want her, she is forced to care for the children born to a mother who does not seem to want them any more than her mother wanted her. The only difference is that the Frau has a husband, and as an upstanding member of society can use and abuse the Child as she sees fit. The Frau is a vicious, heartless woman whose idea of doing her maternal duty is to beat her children with a bundle of twigs. The Child is forced through the fear of punishment to perform an amount of work that would stagger an adult, and is beaten for the smallest infraction. It is highly ironic that a child is forced to be responsible for other children because she has no one to care for her and let her be a child. For the Child, sleep is "a little white road with tall black trees on either side, a little road that led to nowhere, and where nobody walked at all" (91). Sleep is an escape from her tormented life, but she is never allowed to walk on this road because she is always awakened, usually in a violent way by the Frau.

In her helpless rage and frustration, the Child turns upon the only member of the household she can control, a child smaller than herself, and with her immature reasoning, smothers the baby, so that the Frau and the Master will be satisfied, and she can go to sleep. Thus the main conflict in the story is between the Frau, who vents her frustrations with her family and society in beating the Child, and the Child's need to be a child, and to escape the brutality that surrounds her.

"The Advanced Lady"

Mansfield's "The Advanced Lady" is a scalding indictment of so-called "progressive" feminist theories. A self-declared "modern woman" staying at a German pension is used as Mansfield's satirical ruse in this piece. Focusing the story around "the advanced lady's" festive walk with the other residents, including the skeptical English narrator, the narrative takes its course in a series of pretentious discussions held during the journey, with "the advanced lady" serving as the chief pontificator. Mansfield parodies the platitudes of this lady and her "progressive" feminist dialectic and shows how subversive these theories really are. While "the advanced lady" is purportedly working for the benefit of women, she (as representative of these so-called ideals) in reality further promotes their oppression.

The narrator is the only character who sees "the advanced lady" for the superficial idiot she is, and succeeds in demonstrating this to both the audience and perhaps to some extent to this self-proclaimed "modern woman." However, as an

English woman, the narrator is an outsider among the Germans, an exile, and as such her views are held in minimal esteem by her fellow *pensioners*. The Germans criticize everything from Shakespeare to English clothing, and refer to the narrator as their "little English friend" (101). In spite of their subtle innuendoes and condescending remarks, the narrator is successful in forming a deceptive camaraderie with them. She appears calm and amiable in all respects. She observes their customs and emulates their manners, but she politely mocks them without their knowledge of it—"toil(ing) up the stairs of (their) national politeness" (101). She displays interest and curiosity about "the advanced lady" and all that she is reputed to be—"intellectual," "extraordinary"—but she regards neither the lady, nor her society, with respect. Thus, the narrator (as an exile within the group) is able to give the perspective which is necessary for Mansfield's subtle, intricate satirization of "the advanced lady" and her fellow German *pensioners*, to succeed.

Through the narrator's acute sense of perspective one sees that the conflict is based clearly on the ironic disparity between appearance and reality. "The advanced lady" appears "progressive," using all the "right" platitudes, espousing all the "right" views necessary to establish herself as the paradigm for the purely "modern woman." According to "the advanced lady," any woman who considers herself "progressive" should not define herself as one of those "violent creatures who deny their sex and smother their frail wings under the lying garb of false masculinity," but as "the incarnation of comprehending love" (105). She sees herself and all women as "the glad sacrifice of themselves." In reality it is obvious that this woman is not advanced, but rather the most unadvanced of ladies, working to subvert any freedom women might hope to experience by suggesting that frailty and weakness are the criteria for advancement, when in actuality these are the means by which patriarchal society plays upon and oppresses women. The narrator points out the artifice and absurdity of "the advanced lady's" views by suggesting that her theory about women is "as old as the hills—older" (108), that, in fact, it is not new or progressive in any way. "The advanced lady" further informs the narrator that her "ignorance will not go uncontradicted" (108). Thus, Mansfield succeeds in debunking so-called "progressives." She does not accept this kind of ignorance as a means of attaining "progress," and instead calls for a more realistic and comprehensive approach to the advancement of women.

"The Swing of the Pendulum"

In this Mansfield story, the central character, Viola, is interrupted while tending her stove by her landlady who brings a "special letter" to the boarder's room. While there, the landlady orders her to pay the rent before noon the next day or get out. Viola answers curtly, surprising herself with how "calm and indifferent" (110) she feels facing the angry landlady. Alone, Viola opens the letter which comes from her lover Casimir and announces his arrival that afternoon. Her response to the announcement is a mixture of mockery and longing. She crumbles the letter, then moves to her morning toilet, though again a knock interrupts her. Upon answering the knock, her face wet, her underclothes undone, Viola is greeted by a smiling man who says he's looking for a Fraulein Schafer. Viola has never heard of her, but the stranger is slow in leaving. After he's left she falls into a reverie, imagining the stranger as the savior who could end her poverty. Yet she has missed the opportunity by sending him away.

Or has she? After all, she hasn't heard him go downstairs. Pretending to need firewood, Viola leaves her room and finds the stranger smoking a cigarette in the hall. When he invites himself into her room, Viola doesn't object and, in fact, becomes playful as though it were only a game of charades. The stranger offers to send her flowers, which she refuses, and then invites her to go riding, an invitation she accepts, though to Viola it's still only a game. All the while, she observes him and concludes that the man is stupid and silly. He becomes bolder, trying to touch her hair, offering her money in exchange for a kiss, then making a grab for her. Angered, Viola escapes his arms and orders him to leave, but the stranger traps her against the wall. He drags her toward the bed, and Viola only manages to prevent his attack by biting his hand. When he retreats, threatening to tell the landlady, Viola experiences a "sensation of glorious, intoxicating happiness" (118) for winning the battle. Even the anger she felt towards Casimir has disappeared, and she looks forward to his afternoon visit.

Viola, the central character, is an artist possessing a vivid imagination and romantic notions that nearly land her in trouble. Since her lover, Casimir, is searching for an editorial position, we can guess that she too is a writer. Her writer's imagination is evident in the image of "a huge, dream-mountain on which her feet were fast rooted" (110) used to describe her poverty; also later when she imagines a life with the stranger, it appears again. "She began to dream of a wonderful house, and of presses full of clothes and of perfumes" (114). Viola's romantic notions perhaps stem from her imagination. While washing her face in an enamel basin, the thought that women have drowned in buckets leads Viola to experiment, though there's no indication that she seriously means to kill herself. Rather it seems more like a writer's research. A better illustration of her romantic notions comes when Viola considers her future. "There is only one thing I'm fitted for, and that is to be a great courtesan" (113). Her thinking about prostitution might show a character at wit's end, a woman for whom there is no other way of escaping poverty, but Viola is too aware of the dangers—diseases, customers who won't pay—to carry out such a plan.

Besides she has set up too many restrictions ever to become a prostitute, wishing to be a "great courtesan"—not the streetwalker variety—kept in luxury by a wealthy man, such as the stranger smoking in the hall. When Viola tries to act on her notions, by not objecting to the man's entering her room, by playing coy with him, the result is nearly tragic. Although imagination and romantic notions are central to Viola's character, we should also mention another aspect—her inability to tolerate suffering. "I wasn't born for poverty," she says, wishing instead for "ease and any amount of nursing in the lap of luxury" (113). She blames Casimir for their poverty, for although both had unrealistic hopes for their writing, Viola believes Casimir has failed her by not selling his work. Because he is unsuccessful, she despises him and looks for an end to her suffering. Looking for an easy way out leads Viola to her confrontation with the stranger.

Yet despite these characteristics that lead her into trouble, Viola is not a victim. When forced by necessity, she can and does act. Although she spends time worrying about money and even goes so far as to avoid her landlady, Viola is able to answer "shortly" when pressed for the overdue rent. It is as if thinking about a problem is more worrisome than facing it. "...if it came to definite action, with no time for imaginings, her dream-mountain [her poverty] dwindled into a beastly 'hold your nose' affair to be passed by as quickly as possible, with anger and a strong sense of superiority" (110).

In a similar way, with "anger and a strong sense of superiority" (and a strong set of teeth) Viola deals with the stranger who invades her room. After both confrontations she feels a sense of victory, and in the latter fight "a sensation of glorious, intoxicating happiness flooded Viola" (118). As the title suggests, Viola swings like a pendulum between these two aspects of her character—on one side, her romantic nature which is dependent on men and, on the other, her practical nature which is independent, even disdainful, of men. The story's central conflict lies in Viola's inability to balance the two aspects. How can a writer involved in a personal world of imagination survive a day-to-day existence without the support of a man? Conversely, a woman who can foil a would-be rapist, what need does she have for a man? In "The Swing of the Pendulum," however, the conflict is not resolved, just as Mansfield in her own life never seemed to have balanced her dual needs of dependency and independence. In the final paragraph of the story, Viola, as inevitably as a pendulum, swings back to the side of dependency.

"A Blaze"

"A Blaze" traces the development of sexual tensions between the two central characters, Elsa, a married German woman, and Max, her would-be lover. Mansfield ties in a constant feline metaphor within this storyline, making Elsa the cat-like heroine and Max her prey. Mansfield examines the relationship between the men in her story, Victor and Max, by placing them together at the beginning. She then develops the complexity of the storyline by giving Max the opportunity to see Elsa without Victor, Elsa's husband, being present. After the meeting between Elsa and Max, Mansfield then completes her story by showing how Elsa is a master of deception, and is always in control of any situation.

Just like a cat, Elsa is "kept" by her much-older husband, Victor. And also just like a cat, Elsa plays with her prey, Max, for her own gratification before she moves in for the kill. The pivotal action of the story occurs in Elsa's sitting-room. The metaphor of the cat is prevalent in the scene. Elsa is "curled up on the sofa"; her room is "smothered in rugs—an immense tiger skin under the piano—just the head protruding—sleepily savage" (121). Elsa is an incredibly good manipulator. By her phrases and actions she can control the actions of Max. Max is frustrated with Elsa, never knowing how to react to whatever she is going to do. Max's frustration stems from some past actions of Elsa. She had, in the past, "asked me (Max) to pin your flowers on your evening gown...let me come into your bedroom when Victor was out...you pretended to be a baby and let me feed you with grapes" (122). Elsa is a perfect protagonist. She knows what the conventions of society are and how not to violate them. She also knows how to make the men in her life do whatever she wants them to do. She can make seemingly innocent comments and requests which, for Max, have far deeper meaning. She does all of this with such finesse that Max, and for that matter Victor, cannot help but be controlled by her. She is much like a cat in that she will play with something until she tires of it. She will then move on to whatever is next. To Max's reply of what will eventually happen to them, Elsa replies, "I haven't the slightest idea. I never have—just let things occur" (123).

The central conflict in "A Blaze" is quite sexual, and Mansfield presents her characters in such a manner to show that the female has the upper hand. She shows that Max and Victor are good friends. She suggests that the trio has dined together on several occasions and spent time together in other ways. By creating this intricate web within the relationships she can better convey both Max's feelings of frustration and Elsa's method for psychological control over the men in the story. Max wants to make love to Elsa, but she keeps pushing him away. At the point where he divulges his true feelings, Elsa replies, "I am another man's wife" (122). Elsa views herself as an object, or a pet, much like a cat. She says, "I can't help seeking admiration any more than a cat can help going to people to be stroked" (123). Her entire existence seems to be tied in with the men in her life. After Max leaves, Victor returns to comfort his wife, his toy, his possession. He says, "poor darling, your hair's coming down. I'll fix it..."

(123). Just as everything else, Victor will "fix" whatever mess Elsa has made. Elsa knows that Victor will play this role of savior for her; therefore, she acts as she pleases. However manipulative she is, though, she still exists only through the attention of men. She is emotionally immature, but psychologically superior, to the men in the story, making her a perfect heroine.

Chapter Four
Stories from *Bliss and Other Stories* (1920)

After her initial success with *In a German Pension*, Mansfield waited almost an entire decade before publishing her next volume, *Bliss and Other Stories*. *Bliss and Other Stories* was published in London by Constable in 1920, and in New York in 1921. In this second volume, we have a much more polished artist who is gaining a good deal of self-confidence while remaining viciously self-critical. KM had begun to refine her craft of the short story. She was "eager to discover the fulfillment by others of her own ideals" (Alpers 296), and she began to focus primarily on the imagination. *Bliss* was the first volume published after her health had begun to decline drastically. She began to recognize more readily her own mortality, and her themes in *Bliss* are evidence to this. KM had very bleak themes, but in this volume she makes a change in her method. She begins to use daydreams to show the innerworkings of a character's mind. "A characteristic of KM's method is her use of daydreams. In all her later stories, written after *In a German Pension*, she uses it. It becomes an indispensable part of her method" (Friis 128). Also, her recurrent theme of isolation, both isolation of the individual in society and self-induced isolation which occurs in the character's psyche, is prevalent in this volume. "She continues to emphasize what is the distinctive note in her sense of the world—that each person lives to himself or herself alone" (Alpers 299).

The overwhelmingly positive critical reception of this volume surprised even Mansfield. "The critics of its day found *Bliss* a brilliant performance, but the view of life that it seemed to represent was called into question" (Alpers 301). Mansfield was just too bleak and depressing. Her illness had begun to have a great impact on her, and she was growing dissatisfied with her life. Even after the success of this volume, she wrote, "A great part of my book is trivial. It's not good enough" (Alpers 302). She had accomplished her purposes; she had concentrated on the imagination, and she had "discovered the fulfillment by others of her own ideals" (Alpers 296), but she still was not satisfied. Her third volume, *The Garden Party and Other Stories*, was to be the last she published while still alive.

Bliss and Other Stories and *The Garden Party and Other Stories* are the two volumes KM produced as a mature writer. Although Mansfield had not published a book of collected stories since 1911, and had been writing more or less steadily since then, many of the stories in *Bliss*, which was published in December 1920, were only recently completed. For example, "The Man Without a Temperament" was completed in January 1920, and "The Escape" a few months later. Mansfield as a writer was continually working to improve her craft, and her dissatisfaction with some of her work is demonstrated by her decision to leave many earlier stories out of *Bliss*. Mansfield chose to lead off the book with "Prelude," the title suggested by Murry, which had been separately published as a book by the Hogarth Press in 1918, and *"Je ne parle pas français"* which had been published separately by The Heron Press in 1920. These two stories reflect Mansfield's major preoccupations in the book, which are her New Zealand childhood, and the difficult relationships between men and women. The later group includes the previously mentioned "The Man Without a Temperament" which is a thinly veiled jibe at Murry's reluctance to support KM in her illness, and "The Escape," in which a self-absorbed husband, much like Murry, mentally escapes from his demanding wife.

"Prelude"

"Prelude," KM's longest short story, was a lifelong project which has been surrounded by much controversy since her death. Mansfield began writing the story, which was finally published as "Prelude," when she was about 16 and, although she submitted a copy of the story to Leonard and Virginia Woolfe's Hogarth Press for publication, continued working on it intermittently throughout the rest of her life. The development of her working copy, a much longer story called *The Aloe*, can be compared to the development of Mozart's *Requiem* which was also never completed. Perhaps Mansfield identified with Mozart, who also died from tuberculosis and sexually transmitted disease, and never completed "Prelude" because she, like the great composer, felt that completing her major work would hasten her death. Vincent O'Sullivan, however, suggests that (regardless of her fears that her life was intertwined with the completion of the story) she felt compelled to write it. He supports this idea with a quotation from Mansfield's letters, "if I do not write this book I shall die" (Mansfield 175).

O'Sullivan has produced an excellent edition of *The Aloe* and "Prelude" in which Mansfield's manuscripts of *The Aloe* (including passages which she later crossed out) are compared page by page with the published text of "Prelude." O'Sullivan's introduction provides important information about KM's progress on the work, publication of "Prelude" by Hogarth Press, and John Middleton Murry's posthumous publication of *The Aloe* in 1930. O'Sullivan does not directly criticize Murry's treatment of Mansfield's work; however, he does contend that Murry's publication of *The Aloe* contained "the stylistic impositions of another hand." Vincent O'Sullivan's introduction is cautious, and he carefully supports his assertions about Mansfield's work with quotations from her letters and journals, but, like many of Mansfield's critics, he concentrates too much on the details of Mansfield's life and the history of the text, and fails to deal with the content itself.

O'Sullivan does, however, make one very important point about the stories. He quotes Mansfield's desire in her early twenties to write a "sketch, hardly that, more a psychological study," and suggests that *The Aloe* and "Prelude" are examples of this "new way to tell a story" which is "not so much a narrative about events shared by several people, as one where several temperaments unfold in the slantings of perspective, in the tilting gradations of time" (O'Sullivan 25). His point is a valid explanation for the development in "Prelude." Although the experiences of the characters are centered around the move from Wellington to the country, Mansfield's focus is not on the move itself but how each character reacts to it. The children perceive the move as an adventure, yet Linda Burnell seems listless and indifferent. Her sister, Beryl Fairfield, on the other hand, sees it as an end to her chances for freedom through marriage and subsequent financial independence from her brother-in-law.

Stanley Burnell, despite the inconvenient distance from town, is proud of his acquisition, and his mother-in-law is looking forward to the bounty of the country home's gardens.

It is easy to avoid the hidden agendas in Mansfield's work by reading the stories on a superficial level, and this is especially true of "Prelude." Details which seem at first to be contradictory or inadequately developed become frighteningly clear upon a second or third reading. For example, Beryl Fairfield seems to be a beautiful woman desirous of a man, yet inexplicably alone. Upon more careful examination, however, the reader begins to question attractiveness. She admits to acting (even when she is alone), playing flirtatious games (even with her sister's husband), and lying in her letters to friends, and these confessions make her testimony suspect at best; perhaps she is also lying about her personal charm. Beryl, like Rosabel in "The Tiredness of Rosabel," is continually escaping from the reality of her situation by fantasizing about the man who will rescue her, but this is not the only "hidden agenda" in "Prelude." KM uses the length of the story to address several of the themes which usually occur separately in her shorter works—male dominance and insensitivity, female oppression and reinforcement of their own oppression, and lonely, unwanted children.

Stanley, like Daddy in "Six Years After," is a childishly vain man who is proud of his material possessions and insists upon being pampered and having his own way. He expects his mother-in-law to get his slippers for him and demands constant reassurance from his wife that he will not get fat. On the surface, his relationship with Linda seems to be a mutually happy one. Linda curls up in bed with him and urges him, "yes, clasp me" (230) as they fall asleep, and Stanley can't wait to return home from work and see her at the end of the day. But the couple's happiness is suspect, and Linda's thoughts as she walks through the yard ultimately reveal Stanley as a source of anger and resentment. Her attitude towards her children, which has been apparent since the beginning of the story when she says, "we shall simply have to cast them off," suggests a problem which is made brutally clear as she thinks about her feelings during sex, "When she had just not screamed at the top of her voice: 'You are killing me...' For all her love and respect and admiration she hated him"

(258). She does not want the children she has or those Stanley will force her to have in the future, and she hates him for continuing to impregnate her despite her poor health. Stanley's treatment of Linda is inexcusable; yet Linda's refusal to assert herself encourages his thoughtless behavior and reinforces her situation. Linda's festering resentment which she is unwilling or unable to direct towards her husband, unfortunately, manifests itself in her inattention to her children, behavior which is as inexcusable as her husband's behavior towards her.

KM's failure to complete "Prelude" leaves her open to the criticism that she attempted to write a novel and failed; however, "Prelude" stands on its own as a short story, and an open-minded, careful reader will see the eloquence of the work and realize that a novel is not necessary to legitimize her success as a writer. "Prelude" is both an example of Mansfield's ability as an innovative fiction writer, and also an excellent example of KM's insightful and precocious feminist perspective. She possessed an uncanny ability to cut right to the heart of issues and understood, perhaps more fully than many contemporary feminists, that male oppression is not only the fault of sexist, insensitive males, but also the fault of women who allow themselves to be dominated. "Prelude" is noticeably incomplete, and the text of *The Aloe*, as well as letters and journals, provide insight into Mansfield's plans for "Prelude."

"Je Ne Parle Pas Français"

Raoul Duquette, the speaker of KM's confessional monologue, *"Je Ne Parle Pas Français,"* sits in a Parisian cafe and wanders through his past and between fantasy and actuality. The reader can begin immediately to distinguish between Mansfield's Impressionism, "thin, dark girls with silver rings in their ears and market baskets on their arms" (351), and Raoul's superficial ideas, "people are like portmanteaux" (350). Raoul describes himself as a "gentleman, a writer, serious, young, and extremely interested in modern English literature" (362). He reveals himself as a pimp, a neurotic, an effeminate character who can marvel at a woman's suffering and while watching her tears, develop thoughts of the scene's literary possibilities.

The distaste the reader feels for Raoul is increased by his

actions in his Madame Butterfly relationship with Dick, a tweedy English writer, who leaves Raoul after a strange friendship, only to return with Mouse, a stereotypical Englishwoman with a cape and a need for tea, who announces her helplessness and naivete to Raoul with the statement *"Je ne parle pas français."* Dick in turn deserts Mouse to return to his mother. Mouse is deserted finally by Raoul, who recognizes that his shallow nature would not allow him to play the noble protector for very long. Mouse is left completely alone in France, unable to speak that language, and unable to go home because her friends think she is married.

The complex story, one of Mansfield's longest, should be approached with several particulars in mind. The themes of loneliness, homelessness and abandoned love are dealt with in connection with each major character. Raoul says that he has no family, and he severs all human relationships, preferring to observe cafe patrons rather than develop a serious friendship with someone like Mouse. Dick is emotionally unable to continue relationships; he isolates himself from Raoul and Mouse until he is as lonely as the man of the song who sought a dinner. Dick is dependent on his mother. This extreme dependence kills his relationship with Mouse who loves him. Mouse is Madame Butterfly, much more so than Raoul, although he likes to picture himself as Butterfly. Mouse is the true victim, the personification of loneliness, homelessness, and abandoned love.

The limited scope of the characters is important to notice. The characters in the story are treated as stereotypes, not so much by Mansfield as by one another. KM supports this idea of isolation by stereotyping; she names the characters with specific qualities in mind for each of them. *"Je ne parle pas français"* is a summing up of the lack of understanding among characters, "Raoul" is a name that the French associate with homosexuality and cannibalism. Also, "Raoul" is the general name used to mean a cultured man who behaves like an ass. Raoul's surname "duquette" suggests the "coquette" and Raoul's duplicity—what he calls himself in contrast to what he shows himself to be. "Mouse" is a common nickname for women. The name has rather unpleasant connotations: if a woman is the mouse, a man must be the cat. Mouse is limited to her role of submission. Dick's personality in the story is limited because he isolates himself and will not play any role for much length of time, other than his mother's son.

Mansfield's abilities to manipulate a story and leave the reader with a very disturbing impression at the end are striking. She brilliantly shows the well-known concepts of loneliness and homelessness in several different lights. The ideas one has about Raoul, about the cafe Madame, and about Mouse are quite different, although each character seems equally isolated outside human warmth. *"Je ne parle pas français"* is transformed by Mansfield from a "stale little phrase" (353) into an overwhelming statement of loneliness.

"Bliss"

Bertha Young experiences and displays a child-like bliss when in the presence of things—the fruit she's arranged, her baby, the garden's pear tree, the friends who come for dinner, the whole of life. Under the spell of her bliss, Bertha laughs and at times nearly becomes hysterical, for although 30 years old, she behaves like a child. Her surname, Young, suggests this quality, while we can readily find scenes that illustrate Bertha's child-like behavior. Early on she watches Nanny feed her baby, Little Bertha, "like the poor little girl in front of the rich little girl with the doll" (339). Later at dinner she "could have wept with child-like pleasure" (345) when her husband complements the *soufflé*. More importantly to the story, Bertha seems child-like if we examine her sexuality; despite having borne a child, she is sexually immature, unaware, and unresponsive. She loves Harry "but just not in that way" (346), a phrase that hints at an immature attitude wherein sex is a child-bearing duty rather than an expression of love. The line "she'd understood that he was different" (348) indicates that she recognizes her husband's stronger sexual needs, although Bertha cannot respond to his desire. Instead, she is described as "so cold," a reference to frigidity, but it doesn't matter because Bertha believes that being "pals" with her husband is quite enough. Harry, however, takes another view as we discover at the story's end. Giving up sexual intimacy with his wife "had not seemed to matter" to Harry because he has taken a lover, Bertha's new friend, Miss Fulton.

When Harry says in jest, "I never see her, I shan't feel the slightest interest in her until she has a lover" (347), he offers us a clue to the story's thematic puzzle. On a literal level the quotation refers to his child, but since his baby and his wife share the name, Bertha, perhaps by way of analogy Harry is also referring to his spouse. If so, the meaning is clear: Harry will consider Bertha desirable only after a lover has awakened her sexually. The awakening occurs in the story, although in a way unconventional and charged with irony. For only after experiencing a shared sense of bliss with her friend Miss Fulton does Bertha feel passion for her husband. "For the first time in her life Bertha Young desired her husband" (348). Her relationship with Miss Pearl Fulton is central to the story, for Bertha believes her friend shares her feeling of bliss. "You, too?" she wonders. This sharing "does happen very, very rarely between two women. Never between men" (346). It seems ironic that her thoughts of Miss Fulton lead to the arousal of her desire. Bertha wishes to explain her friend to her husband, "What she and I have shared," but the irony, of course, is that both women have shared the same man. A further turn of the screw is that what Harry hints at by way of talking about his "baby"—"I shan't feel the slightest interest in her until she has a lover"—has taken place, accomplished by his own lover.

The two women are linked by more than just what they have shared however; the natural images employed by Mansfield also join Bertha and Pearl inseparably. Bertha is the blooming pear tree in the garden, even clothed in "a white dress, a string of jade beads, green shoes and stockings" to resemble the tree, whereas Miss Fulton is the moon that hangs over the pear tree, "all in silver, with a silver fillet binding her pale blonde hair" (344). Furthermore, her first name—Pearl—suggests the moon's shape and hue just as her fingers "were so pale a light seemed to come from them." Bertha's bliss and her feelings toward Miss Fulton seem to be erotic, and the natural imagery supports this conclusion. "Although it (the pear tree: Bertha) was so still it seemed...to stretch up, to point, to quiver in the bright air, to grow taller and taller as they gazed—almost to touch the rim of the round, silver moon (Miss Pearl Fulton)" (347). Clearly, the tree is phallic, the moon vaginal. If Mansfield intended to suggest a physical love between the women, why did she introduce female *and* male symbols? An answer may lie in Bertha's character. Since she is sexually immature, yet a mother, it seems likely that her sexual experiences have been only with her husband. Perhaps she doesn't recognize the possibility of lesbian lovemaking. Thus, the sexual symbols that intrigue her are the conventional ones for male and female. And even though Miss Fulton arouses erotic feelings in her, Bertha channels her sexual energy back into her marriage and suddenly, for the first time, desires her husband.

At the end, the story moves towards Bertha's self-discovery. She is jolted from her complacent life, her "blissful" satisfaction with the things and people around her, when she discovers that her husband and her friend are lovers. Harry's elaborate show of dislike for Miss Fulton makes the duplicity even worse; he takes every opportunity to disparage her friend, even suggesting that she is "cold like all blond women" (341), when in fact it is his wife whom he finds "cold." Naturally enough, he lies to hide his love affair with Miss Fulton, but won't Bertha, aware of Harry's betrayal, now begin to doubt him regarding other matters? And if her husband can willfully lie to her, what about her servants, her friends? Even her own motives will not be free from suspicion by a Bertha awakened to the possibility of human duplicity. This line of reasoning will throw into shadow every belief she had held to be true. With self-doubt her "childhood" ends, and she enters an adult realm of experience in which a pear tree is merely a tree and not an inspiration for bliss. At the end of the story, though, with one foot on the threshold of adult awareness, Bertha indulges in a final instance of child-like behavior. "Oh, what is going to happen now?" (350) she cries as though the world would stop turning in sympathy with her tragedy. The answer to her question is that nothing will happen. The event, to borrow a line from W.C. Williams, is "a splash quite unnoticed." Mansfield seems to agree when in ending the story she writes "But the pear tree was as lovely as ever and as full of flower and as still" (35).

"The Wind Blows"

"The Wind Blows" explores, with intense subtlety, the power and the beauty of a young pubescent girl on the verge of sexuality. Written in third-person omniscient, the story's narrator moves us expressionistically through young Matilda's morass of sensual awareness. Using the wind as the central metaphor for Matilda's budding sexuality, Mansfield conveys the intensity and uncontrollability of the girl's emerging, and in some ways frightening, identity.

In the story, the young Matilda finds herself at a moment of awakening, of change. The first description—the first line—gives evidence of this: "Suddenly—dreadfully—she wakes up" (214). And, indeed, what has awakened her? The wind—"It is only the wind shaking the house, rattling the windows, banging a piece of iron on the roof and making her bed tremble" (214-15). It is Autumn for Matilda, a time swept by wind, by change. The Summer and her childhood is seen in an ever diminishing state as she finds herself confronting the horizon of her oncoming adulthood—"Summer is over—it is Autumn—everything is ugly" (215). The wind, irrepressible, uncontrollable, overwhelming, frightens Matilda. Her sexuality, with an intensity equalling that of the wind, makes her feel as though her life—at least the life she has always known—"is all over." She is confused and obviously shaken by these growing pangs of indefinable yearning. In fact, every move she makes is marked by her nervous, trembling sensuality. In a private moment "she begins to plait her hair with shaking fingers, not daring to look in the glass" (215).

At her piano lesson with Mr. Bullen "her fingers tremble so that she can't undo the knot in the music satchel…It is the wind" (215). Her perceptions are filled with erotic awareness, as well. She notices Marie Sawinson, her neighbor, running in the garden as "her skirt flies up above her waist; she tries to beat it down…but it is no use—up it flies" (215). The "wind" controls everything she perceives. She notices every physical movement, every subtle gesture. When watching her piano teacher, Mr. Bullen, she observes that "He turns the page slowly. She watches his hand—it is a very nice hand and always looks as though it has just been washed" (217). She looks in the mirror with her brother, Bogey, and sees "they have the same excited eyes and hot lips" (218).

The character's conflict is found in a raging inner struggle between familiar childhood innocence and inevitable sexual experience. The "wind" and its power, its force, is sweeping her toward discovery; a discovery she does not completely understand, but trepidly anticipates. She is scared of herself and of this awareness—"the wind, the wind. It's frightening to be here in the room by herself. The bed, the mirror.... It's the bed that's frightening. There it lies sound asleep" (217). But, Matilda's bed, and her previously sleeping sexuality, is now awakening. Her childhood is passing behind her, already fading, as she hears the clock chiming in the distance "for the last time," reminding her that this period of her life is over. She sees a vision of herself and her brother, Bogey—children together on the beach—fading as "the dark stretches a wind over the tumbling water. They can't see those two (themselves) anymore. Good-bye, good-bye" (219). Accepting the inevitable change, she lingers over the passing familiarity of childhood, promising herself, in the end, not to forget this time in her life as she moves toward adulthood.

"Psychology"

In the short story "Psychology," a reader is confronted with an unnamed couple in their thirties who are supposedly past and above the "stupid emotional complications" (316) passion would induce in their relationship. Yet, it is this suppression of their emotions and passion that causes their mental anguish. Throughout the evening, they play psychological games with each other as they try, while their excitement rages within, to be the sophisticated, reserved intellectuals they consider themselves. The unpleasant and frustrating evening ends with him leaving without either of them having made any progress towards the goal both secretly desire. After embracing the older virgin, the woman's attitude suddenly changes to one of contentment. She writes a pleasant note to the man, ending it with the same endearing words she spoke to the virgin.

Mansfield uses light and darkness, quickness and slowness to represent the couple's conflicting emotions. The bright, "fluttering fire" and its flames represent the passion they are trying so desperately to control. Yet, they feel safe in the light; an unfamiliar, "boundless, questioning dark" (317) lurks outside the brightness. At the times their fervor is unbearable, everything speeds up. They get frantic, think faster, but they demand self-control. And it is this self-control which keeps them from expressing their true feelings, resulting in strained silence. Two other symbols are the old virgin and the dead violets. If the woman continues to deny her feelings she could become this pathetic, lonely virgin, and her youth and appearance could become like the withered flowers. Once she realizes this, the woman releases her emotions though an intimate embrace, equating it with the one she avoided with the man. She is then freed from her troubling anxieties.

The woman in this story could easily be Mansfield because she, herself, decided to express her own passion and true feelings even though society pressured her to do otherwise. Furthermore, her preference concerning the subject matter in her works comes out through the couple's conversation about psychological literature. Irony exists in the fact that the couple discusses the resolution of hidden conflicts while acting in opposition to their words. Again Mansfield criticizes men's inadequacies and insensitivity as the woman appreciates the beautiful night, knowing the man will never even notice—as indeed he never does. Mansfield perhaps uses this story to express her own feelings and fears, and as a moral message to criticize society's superficial games and some possible results.

"Pictures"

Mansfield's satirical "Pictures" offers a brutal picture of life for the aging entertainer. In order to pay her rent, Miss Ada Moss must find work as an actress. The narrator describes Ada's day-long search for a job, which becomes more and more desperate as she travels from talent agency to talent agency. In the narration of Ada's search, Mansfield creates a harsh world of competition that Ada must face. She is confronted by multitudes of competing actress, all of whom seem to be younger, and there are far too few roles for far too many people. The portrayal of Ada as such a pitiful, desperate character makes "Pictures" a haunting story for those who fear growing older.

Miss Ada Moss, the main character, is a struggling performer. She apparently achieved some success at a younger age as a contralto singer, but is now struggling simply to survive. From the narration, the reader can see that Ada is a natural performer. Through the narrator, the reader sees that Ada is constantly playing some sort of role. The text is covered with descriptions of Ada's pose or Ada's expression at a given moment: "She put her head on one side and smiled vaguely at the letter." "This letter seemed to afford her peculiar satisfaction" (393-94). When Ada steps out of the house to begin her job search, it seems as if the narrator is describing a new character in the story: "Ten minutes later, a stout lady in blue serge...sang in a low contralto voice..." (395). This use of such an impersonal reference causes the reader some confusion. Who is this lady? Is it Ada? However, the confusion then leads the reader to sense that Ada has put on her "guise." She is playing the role of the star just waiting to be discovered. Many people, however, see through Ada's performances, and see her for what she is, a tired, desperate person who needs a job. Mansfield's use of descriptive language helps portray Ada as a dramatic role player. Ada does not only place herself in roles, she views the world in dramatic terms as well. "Here, she (the landlord) nodded, mysteriously...Here her voice rose.... And here it fell, sepulchral" (395). With these descriptions, Mansfield presents the landlord as Ada sees her, a character in a horror movie.

The conflict, then, in "Pictures" is a familiar one. Ada is struggling to stay young in a world where youth is a prerequisite. No one wants to hire her; no one even notices her. The competition is too great. Throughout the story, the reader sees Ada living off her past successes and growing ever more desperate to keep on the mask of youth, symbolically represented by Ada's powder puff, described by the narrator as "old" and "dead" (394). Perhaps we see in this story the fears of Mansfield, who was always a natural performer herself. When Ada looks in the mirror, she sees an ugly face, frowning back at her. This face doesn't seem to fit in with the way Ada tries to project herself. In this way, Mansfield seems to be giving the reader a clue to her own insecurities. In the end, Ada does seem to find a way to survive for a while. At least she finds shelter for the night, as Mansfield juxtaposes the act of auditioning with getting picked up at a bar. This rather interesting comparison serves to reinforce the notion that Ada is trying desperately to keep the guise of the young, attractive girl waiting to be discovered.

"The Man Without a Temperament"

While staying with his terminally ill wife in an Italian resort, Robert Salesby has found himself trapped in a stagnant environment, and he too has become as stagnant as the setting and the characters surrounding him. He is losing the ability to react emotionally to anything at all as his nagging, increasingly dependent wife diminishes any hope for rejuvenation. Mansfield provides a plot structure and reveals the main character's dying temperament through two main devices: first, she has written the story almost entirely in Mr. Salesby's point of view; second, this limited omniscience allows Mansfield to open the protagonist's memory through flashbacks, presenting a contract between his stagnant present and his idyllic past in London—a time when he still adored his attractive, enthusiastic wife.

Thus, the story as a whole remains confined to the present, as the characters inhabiting the resort live solely for the moment, sensing no future possibilities. The past exists only in fading fragments within Mr. Salesby's mind; but even there memory is merciless, reminding him of the irreversible decay of his spirit as he consigns his potentially healthy life to caring for his demanding but devoted invalid wife.

Without a doubt, Mr. Salesby would like to end his marriage and return to England. Mansfield reveals his anxiety from the beginning when she describes him "turning the heavy signet ring upon his little finger" (412), feeling trapped in a cumbersome marriage. He turns the ring habitually whenever he is waiting for Mrs. Salesby—a symbolic waiting, as he also waits for his wife to die. But while he waits, the characters around him assume morbid animals form in his mind. He sees the Topknot couple "rooting in a tin full of paper shavings for pieces of speckled fruit" (412). Then, "Their two coils of knitting, like two snakes, slumbered beside their tray" (412). To Mr. Salesby the plush resort environment is hellish for its sterility; even the flowers in the garden which should seem beautiful when blooming seem stagnant, decaying, "as if exhausted" by the tedium of waiting. Mr. Salesby feels no pleasure at this resort because he has no intrinsic desire to help or love his wife. When his wife first appears, she asks him to move his chair closer to hers; he refuses, indicating for the first time that he feels no affection for her. That affection is as near death as is Mrs. Salesby. Years earlier Mr. Salesby's affection flourished, but he now suffers under the torment of remembering that past affection.

By presenting the story from Mr. Salesby's point of view, Mansfield depicts a selfish man unable to appreciate the condition of a woman severely limited by her failing health. But while Mr. Salesby remains tied to a woman he cannot bring himself to love, Mrs. Salesby remains as devoted to her husband as ever, and she holds as much of the youthful innocence and vivaciousness as her feeble body will allow. To reveal this conflict, Mansfield resorts to shifting the point of view briefly: Mrs. Salesby gazes on her husband with desire and admiration after the couple has seen three girls bathing.

Still, in the end, Mansfield does not place her sympathy clearly with either character; while Mrs. Salesby clings stubbornly to the emotional residue of past happiness, Mr. Salesby feels deprived of the advantages of his healthy body, leashed unfairly to a dead marriage when he should fulfill his own desires. Neither character deserves condemnation—only pity; both suffer in a devotion that equals death. As Mr. Salesby whispers at the end, he secretly views his unceasing devotion as "rot" (425). Perhaps the cruelest thought of all is that when his wife dies, he may once again feel liberated.

"Mr. Reginald Peacock's Day"

In "Mr. Reginald Peacock's Day," Mansfield details the vanity, shallowness, and selfishness about a vocal teacher who manipulates and then proceeds to interpret each encounter throughout the day as evidence of his own artistic superiority. As he bathes and dresses, he "thrills with satisfaction" (386) at his mirror image. His morning ritual with his son reflects mannerisms that he copied from an aristocratic family. Disdain is expressed for his wife who *claims* to enjoy housework rather than train a servant.

Each encounter with three adoring female pupils prove to Mr. Peacock that he is not only a gifted artist and a potential lover, but he is a great teacher of the world in the ways to "escape from life." After dining with an admirer who had written him, Mr. Peacock sipped champagne with Lord Timbuck, who also acknowledged

Mr. Peacock's persuasive artistical talents by treating him as an equal and refusing to call him "Mr. Peacock." His triumphant evening ended with the crash of his boot as he prepared to befriend his wife in bed. Ironically, superficiality arose again, and he uttered the same trite expression that he so often used with his students, "Dear Lady, I should be so charmed" (390).

Reginald Peacock, the central character in this story, is an indulgent man who enjoys all activities centered on himself. He is a subtle braggart, who believes that he is not vain, for "he couldn't stand vain men" (386). Mr. Peacock sees himself as an excellent provider who never reproached his wife for her lack of funds, yet he doles out a mere 10 shillings for her for the dairy bill. He refuses to admit that his wife is without a servant because of his selfishness; no doubt past servants found him too difficult to please. Surely, his wife knows his temperament and his mannerism and accepts the household responsibilities because "it makes life...peaceful" (377). Mr. Peacock enjoys the adulation of his female students, and he maintains a seductive aura as he conducts his singing classes.

Clearly, Mr. Peacock's struggle is internal; he actually believes that what he thinks and what he says is right. He is so vain, so artificial. As the story gradually unfolds, there are constant conflicts as he perceives that his wife gloats over the way she awakens him each morning; his son, Adrian, is not really agreeable to this aristocratic greeting between father and son each morning; and Adrian wonders why his father must "always sort of sing to him instead of talk" (386); Peacock struggles with Miss Brittle as he convinces her to "practise before a glass"; the Countess Wilkowska wants to sing songs instead of exercises and cannot meet his approval with "You love me.... Yes, I *know* you love me!" (390) until, of course, she agrees to sing with him.

Miss Marian Morrow is quite depressed when she arrives for her lesson. He offers to listen to her problem, but he decides that it will be better to sing to her. She welcomes his singing with excessive flattery. The major conflict occurs when Mr. Peacock decides to befriend his wife. He is quite drunk "staggering home," and, upon his arrival, he decides that his wife should adore and praise his talents just as his pupils and Lord Timbuck. However, his wife fails to react to the excessive admiration he receives and welcomes from others. In his final effort "to win her," he realizes his shallowness, for he can only utter his usual trite expression—"Dear lady, I should be so charmed—so charmed!"

"Sun and Moon"

"Sun and Moon" is a very different story. Sun and Moon are children. And it is through children's eyes that they witness preparation for their parents' party. Sun and Moon are properly consumed by the array of delicacies to be had at the evening's celebrations—elaborate orchestrations of hams, jellies, fish, and an ice pudding, of course. It is all quite splendid and fascinating until the children are marched off to the nursery and prepared, rather like the food, for their cursory appearance. At length, Sun and Moon make their appearance and are sent back upstairs where children belong. And certainly, they try to sleep. As hard as curious children may, but enthrallment with mystic pursuits wins in the end. Sun and Moon are discovered at the top of the stair, taken below amid Mother's protests, and offered leftovers. Leftovers do not at all command the magic, elegance, and structure of unviolated dinner. Moon, the daughter, eats passively. Sun, the son, stomps off to the nursery shattered and betrayed.

This is a parable of dualities, of pairs of relationships that do and do not work: Mother and Father, Sun and Moon, upstairs (the world of innocence), downstairs (that of experience), reality, imaginative experience, confidence, and deceit. The essential conflicts are those among these sets of pairs. All the characters are necessarily flat and, for parable purposes, remain mostly unchanged at the end of the story. Except for Sun. When Sun sees the melted ice pudding, he suffers a significant personal loss; the ideal world is corrupted, his fantasy compromised. It is appropriate that Sun, the older child, can feel the weight of this metaphor while Moon remains nicely in the dark.

This story has, besides its obvious dialogue between reality and fantasy, much to say about how we rate our expectations of Truth against our fear of Lies. It is worth noting that the principle force sustaining the narrative line is nothing more complex than that very same fear. Simple and harrowing. Ah, noble parable, you are a too-slighted form. So we wait. And Mansfield's treatment of an ending that is both climax and anti-climax strikes a reader as the real achievement of the story. But the most interesting feature about the story is Mansfield's refusal to allow an affirmative reading of the parable. She leaves us only with a terminal tableau and a resonating nervous energy between our illusory world and our world of quantifiable circumstance, the difference between which is the difference of this and that, you and me, dark and light, Sun and Moon.

"Feuille d'Album"

Katherine Mansfield's *"Feuille d'Album"* is an ironic and satirical story about a young painter named Ian French. Ian, who enjoys solitude in the privacy of his own home, becomes the "talk of the town" when three women, on separate occasions, try to enter his private life to help him find love. The first woman pays Ian a visit at his home to see if she can grant him some motherly care, but when she rings the doorbell, Ian does not answer. A second woman tries to capture his heart by leaning over him so that he may smell the fragrance of her perfume and become enthralled by it. Later that evening she rings his doorbell, but Ian does not answer. A third woman invites him to a club for drinks and dancing with hopes that later he will invite her to his apartment. To her surprise, not only does he not invite her up to his apartment, but he tells her "good night" in the street. In the final analysis, all of these women's efforts are hopeless in helping Ian find love; however, all hope is not gone because one day Ian finds love on his own.

Ian French, the central figure in the story, is a talented, young painter whose outer appearance causes people to think he is an abandoned or run-away child. Quite the contrary, Ian lives in a beautiful apartment on the top floor of his complex where his view affords him great outdoor sceneries. He doesn't leave his studio, which is located in his apartment, too often. This is why his private life is such a mystery. Even though his clothes lack the appearance of one who is talented and ingenious, Ian is just the opposite of what others perceive him to be. He keeps everything in his studio "as neat as a pin." His entire kitchen is arranged to form an image of "still life," and just above his bed is a small, neatly painted picture that reads: GET UP AT ONCE. However, no one knows about this side of Ian's personal life because he never allows anyone to enter his studio.

The conflict, which is the irony in the story, takes place when Ian finds love on his own. One day while he is sitting eating prunes and throwing the stones over the balcony, his eyes are caught by the presence of a beautiful, young girl who is carrying a pot of daffodils, but all of a sudden the girl disappears. Later she returns to the window dressed in a dark pinafore, but this time she is talking to someone. Ian never sees anyone at the window other than the girl, so he concludes that her mother must be an invalid and her father deceased. In attempts to get to know this girl, Ian imagines that he sees the two of them together in her home. Through his imagination, he sees the two of them arguing, and he concludes that this girl has a bad temper.

When he tries to show her his painting, he finds that she has no admiration for his work. Does what Ian imagines discourage him? Absolutely not. Ian is convinced that this is the perfect girl for him. In attempts to meet her, one day Ian decides to follow her to the grocery store. He watches how carefully she selects her groceries, and he is most fascinated by her composure during the whole shopping process. To Ian, her composure is sending out a message to him, one that says the two of them are tired of living in a grown-up world, and that they are the only two people who are the same age. After receiving this message, Ian is more positive than ever that this is the only girl for him. With persistence, he continues to follow the girl to her doorstep where he finally makes his big move. When he gets the opportunity to approach her, instead of him asking her for her name or even better, a date, he says "Mademoiselle, you dropped this" (330), and gives her an egg he purchased earlier. Poor Ian—back to square one.

"A Dill Pickle"

In her short story entitled "A Dill Pickle," Katherine Mansfield sets up a series of binaries in order to tell her story. By using this system of juxtaposition, Mansfield shows the two sides of her argument, and the audience can better understand the choices made by the two characters in the story. The action of the story begins six years after the two characters had last parted. By the end of the story, the audience learns that the two had once been intimately involved with each other. This relationship had been terribly one-sided, a fact that six years had not changed. Mansfield gives the audience the ideas of past versus present, of sweet versus sour as it relates to the couple's relationship, of innocence versus experience within the psyche of each individual character, of both interior and exterior views of the characters (both literally and symbolically), and of dreams versus reality.

The central character of the story is a young female whose name is Vera. She is very introspective and introverted. When she first sees the male character, she "opens up." He has a way of creeping into her psyche which no one else has ever been able to do. When the reader first encounters this character, he is peeling an orange in that "special" way, the way that only he can. His method of peeling an orange, or getting inside of something in order to get to what is good, is symbolic in the story. After the initial meeting she "raised her veil and unbuttoned her high fur collar" (336), thereby exposing herself to him. After a good amount of banter, Vera begins to see how things have not changed in the past six years. Although she loves him, he still is a controlling, manipulative person. She seems to have gained a good amount of self-confidence in the past six years, and she is unwilling to relinquish this. At the beginning of the conversation, she remembers the dreams they both had of visiting faraway places together.

It is interesting to note how Mansfield employs two daydream sequences, both of which are experienced by the central characters. In the first sequence, Vera daydreams about one day she and the man were on a lawn. A little girl in a white dress appears, symbolic of youth and innocence; the girl she once was. After he destroys both her and her dreams, she "saw the pale dress of the woman outspread and her folded parasol, lying on the grass like a huge pearl crochet hook" (334). All of her innocence is now gone because she has finally seen the man for what he is. In the story, the reader sees the affirmation of what Vera already knew. In order for her to be a real person, she had to rid herself of someone who was literally controlling her life.

The central conflict within the story is love. Vera loves the man, but he cannot return this love. She has never loved anyone like she loves him. They are both beneficial for each other, but if she is ever to remain true to herself, she much rely on herself totally and dismiss him. Only he can see inside her; only she understands and listens to him. For him, this relationship is purely selfish; for her, selfless. In the six years, she had created a wall so no one could hurt her again. For a brief moment, he destroyed the wall, but she rebuilt it. She had unveiled herself to him once more, and once more he disappointed and destroyed her. He laughed at the letter she had written to him. It is safe to infer that she had written her true feelings in this letter. When he dismissed these feelings as folly, she finally knew that he could not ever return her feelings of love. The metaphors in this story really help to create it. Her memories of him were sweet, just as the orange fruit was sweet, but the reality that existed and still does exist is as bitter as the dill pickle for which the story was named.

"The Little Governess"

"The Little Governess" is a story about a young English governess who traveled alone to Germany. She made this trip during the night-time, as recommended by a lady at the Governess Bureau. Despite an early warning, the young governess dropped her protective shield and allowed an elderly gentleman she met on the train to become her friend. She even accepted this seemingly kind gentleman's offer to escort her on a tour of Munich which ended abruptly because he physically forced himself on her.

Male dominance is clearly seen in this story. The first man the little governess encountered was the porter who asserted himself on her by carrying her dress-basket despite her refusal of his services. To punish her for an unsatisfactory tip, he turned what should have been a safe "Ladies Compartment" into a room open to anyone. The second man she met was an older gentleman who manipulated her into his bachelor's flat where he forced an unwelcome kiss to her lips. Finally, the waiter at the German hotel refused to help her when she was at a point of hysteria. The governess was consumed by men just as she consumed the strawberries given to her on the train.

The governess's journey out of England is Mansfield's own biographical journey out of New Zealand. Set during the night-time, darkness in this story forewarns of danger. White images, such as the "white steps into the white road to the hotel" (211), represent safety. She would have been safe if she had stayed at the hotel where she was supposed to wait for Frau Arnholdt. During her tour of Munich the rain forced the governess close to the old man as they shared an umbrella. The dark ice cream and finally the dark passage up to the old man's flat all forewarn of the imminent danger which did indeed follow. Mansfield's use of light and dark imagery in this story portrays safety and danger, respectively.

"Revelations"

This story consists of a day in the "life" of the rich, but unhappy, Monica Tyrell: from her inconvenient awakening at 9:30, to face a windy day, to her inevitable lunch at Prince's at 1:30. Small awakenings or revelations present themselves amid the rituals of her day, but each time her circumstances shut the door that would lead to freedom.

Monica is oppressed by wealth. Like the recurring image of wind in the story, the rituals of Monica's life force her in meaningless directions. Consciousness of her own aging process causes her to "suffer from her nerves" (425). She wallows in circumstances which hold her just beyond the reach of freedom. When she gets her first revelation, her first glimpse of freedom, the narrator says that she owns the world, but then, perhaps by way of correction adds, "no, no, she belonged to no one but Life" (427). For Monica, to own is equivalent to being owned. She can't belong to Life while everything that makes up her life belongs to her. This illustrates a teaching older than Mansfield which says to "be on guard against every form of greed for not even when one has an abundance does his life consist of his possessions" (from the *New Testament*).

Monica seems to catch sight of this truth for a moment, and reacts by racing off through town. But even here, her familiar tendencies rule as she soars to the beauty shop "letting herself be hurled back and forth" (428) in the car, oblivious to the Life of the "cold, cross-looking" driver. Her friendship with George and Madame would seem to be the more wholesome, less selfish side of her life. Yet, while they perhaps understand her, she gives little to them aside from her regular patronage. This is well established as Monica's soaring mood nose-dives under the sad, gloomy atmosphere of the shop. She snaps at George for his absentmindedness. In the end, George confides the information of his little girl's death to Monica. Monica flees in the only direction she knows: to Prince's. When she sees a flower shop, another door to freedom is in view. She can give someone else the understanding for which she longs, and thus step out from the force of the wind. But, as the driver fails to hear her tap of the glass, she finds herself, instead, at Prince's to meet her habit, Monsieur.

Each occurrence, character, and phrase in this story was so carefully chosen as to make this not just a story, but a plea for the sake of the oppressed. Hope rises in the reader each time Monica has a revelation that would lead to freedom. And, in the end, we are left to wonder if Monica will have other chances to be free, and if she will ever be freed.

"The Escape"

"The Escape" is a story about an English couple who are on holiday in France. The wife is shrewish and discontented, not so much with traveling as with her husband's inability to handle the situations which arise to her satisfaction. They miss the train because her husband does not demand that the hotel bill be produced immediately, and are forced to take a carriage over a hot and dusty road to catch the train in the next town. The husband is an affable man who does not let the inevitable delays of traveling bother him. He enjoys the carriage ride, trying to make the best of the situation, and does what he can to calm his wife's nerves and soothe her fretful nature. He acquiesces to her every whim by not giving money to the children who surround the carriage, and puts away his cigarettes because the smoke upsets her. Finally, after one particularly nasty bump, the wife's parasol is jogged out of the carriage, and she, in a fit of pique, goes to fetch it herself. Her husband, left in peace for a few moments, has an epiphany while staring at a tree and hearing a woman's voice floating on the breeze. Later on, having caught the train they had been hoping to catch, the husband stands outside on the breezeway hearing his wife complain as usual, but feeling a "heavenly happiness" (436).

The husband is the featured character in "The Escape" because he is intelligent and sensitive enough to undergo a change, while the wife remains static. The story is structured in such a way that it opens from the point of view of the wife, who is feeling put-upon and is mocking the way her husband handled the bill at the hotel and his instructions to the driver to *"Allez, vite, vite."* Everything that goes wrong is her husband's fault, everyone is out to torment her, and her sensitive nerves are about to snap. She begins to cry in self-pity, and opens her purse to find her scented handkerchief. It is at this moment that the husband appears, noting the contents of his wife's purse, and commenting to himself, "In Egypt she would be buried in those things" (432). From this comment, the reader understands that the husband is awed by his wife; she is as autocratic and imperious as Cleopatra. We can also note his unconscious desire to be rid of her. In reality, his wife is a castrating bitch, wielding her precious parasol as her phallic substitute for the one thing she has removed from her husband. She is certain that he gets a malicious thrill out of making things difficult for her. She is utterly blameless, and therefore holds all power in the relationship. Her husband, who seems resigned to the fact that he is stuck with this woman as his wife, does his best to be calm and reasonable in the face of such abuse, but his wife's ironic comment that "if I don't escape you for a minute I shall go mad" (434), touches off in her husband the realization that he will go mad as well if he doesn't escape from his wife, for he feels hollow, parched, and withered, a man of ashes. It is then when his epiphany comes.

The major conflict in "The Escape" is not the obvious one between the husband and the demand of his dissatisfied wife, but is the conflict within the mind of the husband. He wants to love his wife and to make her happy, yet some small secret inside him knows that he has made a hideous mistake in marrying this shrew, and that no power on earth can make her happy. The story outlines his struggle to understand his wife, to keep the spark of love alive, but in his moment of peace away from his wife, he realizes that the struggle has depleted him, and he has nothing more to give to his wife. He notices the tree, and gives himself up to the peace and silence of its immense size and its leaves blotting out the sky. He hears a woman's voice come to him, "untroubled," and "soft, dreaming, gentle" (435).

The imagery Mansfield employs when the husband's peace is shattered by this voice is of a man drowning. He resists the dark idea that comes pushing up in his breast; it is "warm, stifling," like water rising over his head, this idea is a "weed," unfamiliar, faintly sinister, the idea that he need no longer care for his wife, that he could simply give up his struggle to please her, not because he has failed, but because she has. "Deep, deep, he sank into the silence, staring at the tree and waiting for the voice that came floating, falling, until he felt himself enfolded" (436). The husband has effected an escape from his wife, has gone to a place where her voice is indistinct, as though heard through water, and where peace reigns.

Chapter Five
Stories from *The Garden Party*
and Other Stories (1922)

The Garden Party and Other Stories was published by Constable on 23 February 1922, and in New York later that year. After having already published two largely successful volumes, what could Mansfield possibly have wanted to do? KM wanted to demonstrate her maturity as an artist. She still felt a need to be accepted by the public, and she wanted to exhibit what she viewed as perfection in her own work. Whereas in *Bliss* she had concentrated on the imagination, she now wanted to write about feeling. She also wanted to show a more positive outlook on life, and for her to do this, she had to focus on childhood. The stories in *The Garden Party and Other Stories* are much brighter than the others KM had written. It seems strange but true that as her health declined, her stories brightened. She began to withdraw into herself, and, "like Wordsworth, invalided and isolated, she nurtured her youthful experience and made it the center of her work in her later fiction. The depiction of children—herself and those she had known—became her trademark" (Magalaner 122). Although her later fiction has a large emphasis on children, her primary emphasis is on the interpersonal relationship between characters. She writes, in this volume, a good deal about feeling in these interpersonal relationships. Magalaner remarks that "a heightened sensitivity to personal relationships in fiction is perhaps Mansfield's foremost asset as a writer of short stories" (Magalaner 125).

The Garden Party and Other Stories continues Mansfield's interest in exploring her New Zealand childhood, but new themes are introduced in some of the stories, and KM's outlook has also changed. Death plays an important role in stories such as "The Garden Party" and "A Voyage." Portraits of women on their own also figure prominently in *The Garden Party* such as "Miss. Brill,"

72

and "The Daughters of the Late Colonel." But Mansfield's outlook on her characters has changed somewhat from *Bliss*. "Harsh lines have disappeared, and all the characters save one are described with love or pity" (Alpers 305). Mansfield, during the year she worked on stories for *The Garden Party*, felt much more settled and secure in her relationships with Murry and LM. This in turn helped her to move away from the cynicism and bitterness that marked her earlier work. KM chose to lead off *The Garden Party* with "At the Bay," a continuation of "Prelude" and a signal to the reading public that Mansfield placed real importance on her New Zealand stories.

All the stories in this volume were published between 1920 and 1921. This was known as the most productive period of Mansfield's writing career. About these stories Cherry Hankin wrote, "They have a certain ineffable quality about them partly because, as her hold on life weakened, so the intensity of her artistic vision heightened" (Hankin 12). Of the 15 stories in this collection, 10 are set in England or the Continent and five in New Zealand. The reviews this volume received were highly critical. *The English Review* wrote, "the book is cruel, passionless and cynical." And though Robert Littell and Conrad Aiken noted her remarkably skillful diction and style, they also had reservations about the narrow and somewhat superficial themes included. Malcolm Cowley wrote against *The Garden Party* as well. However, today most serious readers tend to favor the KM stories in this volume.

"At the Bay"

"At the Bay" follows one family through a normal day of life. The story divides into 13 sections, each of which is an episode that provides a statement about society. The sections also introduce the various members of the family, and offer insight into the characters' present situation and the dreams of his/her youth.

The conflict centers on the characters succumbing to social expectations. This process is best explained by focusing on one character. Linda, as a wife and mother, has met every social obligation demanded of her; however, she sacrificed her own dreams and desires in the process. She abandoned the dream of traveling to marry a man she loves only sometimes. She bore three children for whom she feels cool affection. Her present existence consists of talking to people. Linda has no more dreams; therefore, she falls further into the whirlpool of social requirements, one of which is submission. This theme is less obvious in the story as a whole, but it nonetheless makes a strong impression. For example, the women cater to Stanley's every whim; however, when he is gone they are happy. By showing the fate of Linda and the other characters, Mansfield establishes that the individual controls his/her destiny and only the individual can free oneself from dominance of any kind.

From the constrictive atmosphere of the story, Mansfield creates a champion of hope. Beryl, Linda's sister, is a unique character. She still has the dream that her perfect love will appear someday; however, she is not naive to the ways of the world. Beryl uses this knowledge and does not settle for the advances of a married man. She does not compromise what she believes and she does not allow others to compromise her. Beryl is set apart from other Mansfield characters as a fighter instead of a victim.

"The Garden Party"

Laura Sheridan feels as wonderful as the day is perfect—the perfect day for the perfect garden-party, and the excitement and anticipation for this event fill young Laura with a glow comparable to that of the sun's beaming down upon Laura. But in "The Garden Party," a dark cloud moves over Laura as she learns that a man down the lane has died. Regardless of her attempts to stop it, the garden party goes on as planned, and even though she was deeply worried about how they could have a party after knowing someone had died, she thoroughly enjoys herself. Afterwards, Laura carries a basket of leftovers to the dead man's family where she sees him against the dark, eerie backdrop of his surroundings. This encounter with death, after an afternoon abounding with life and all its pleasures, provides Laura with her first lesson about the discrepancy between life's apparent rationality and its actual absurdities. Mansfield uses this contradiction of life and death in simultaneity as a basis for this story.

One side of the contradiction concerns growth and "life." Laura begins "to grow beyond the garden" (546) and her family.

Her feelings for her father and brother, the workmen, and even the dead man show her deviation from her own sex, her mother, and sisters. Laura enjoys herself most when she is prowling around forbidden places with her brother Laurie. Her mother concerns herself only with "garden" affairs, while Laura worries about class distinctions, natural phenomena for Mrs. Sheridan. Laura would rather have these "extraordinarily nice workmen...for friends...than the silly boys" (536) she knows. (Her intentions are noble yet she is still patronizing in her thoughts towards the workers.) Another illustration of the emerging differences between her and other female members is that Laura feels horribly distraught over the death of the man down the lane, but her sisters and mother think her reactions to something so remote are ridiculous. Her mother tells her she is absurd and that "people like that don't expect sacrifices...that would spoil everyone's enjoyment" (543). This divergence from her mother represents her developing maturity and her escape from childhood.

Other aspects of the story symbolize Laura's growth; for example, the roses, almost intentionally, bloom for the party. The afternoon "slowly ripened, slowly faded, slowly closed its petals" (545). And finally, Laura views the corpse, with its head sunk into the pillow and his eyes closed, as if he were a flower that had reached its end of the growth cycle. These descriptions parallel Laura's own growth. In contrast to these representations of growth and life, a few instances link the garden-party, in all its wonder, to death. For instance, the white arum lilies are funeral flowers. The black hat and daisies represent life and death commingling. And Jose's depressing song seems totally ironic considering the circumstances in which it's sung. These instances serve as warnings for what the reader shall soon understand.

When the afternoon begins to fade into darkness, the other side of the contradiction begins to come into light. Laura leaves the afternoon of glorious sunshine, stylish people, and fancy cream puffs and enters a world of darkness and shadows of big dogs. She is not a part of the lane's world; in the smoky night her frock shines while the obscure inhabitants of this supernatural dimension stop talking to watch her, silently. The evening journey absolutely contrasts with her afternoon party. Her walk down the lane seems to symbolize an inward voyage of discovery into undiscovered areas of herself. Guided by a sordid "little creature," she is taken to the corpse which she describes in terms that totally contradict the actual scene: "remote, so peaceful" and "wonderful, beautiful" and "happy" (548). She realizes that the garden-parties and lace frocks are not all that is important; there is more, much more. Laura learns, as life and death join when she sees the dead man, that life includes death. Immediately after leaving the corpse, Laura is not exactly sure what she has learned about life, but she has come to terms with the confusing mixed aspects of her existence.

"Mr. and Mrs. Dove"

Mansfield, in her "Mr. and Mrs. Dove," offers the reader an account of a marriage proposal from the potential groom's point of view. This proposal is an incredibly stressful event for Reggie, the potential groom, and is seen by him as an attempt that is almost certainly futile. The object of Reggie's affections is a young woman named Anne, a silly little girl, really, who can do nothing but giggle when she is near Reggie and who seems to dream that someday some handsome young prince will come and take her away. During their conversation Reggie seems to be constantly trying to keep up with Anne. Even though she giggles quite often, she seems to be in control of the conversation and the situation; Reggie always seems to be following her lead in one way or another. From their actions, it is easy to see that Anne's comparison of them to her doves is an accurate one. According to Anne, "Mrs. Dove...gives that little laugh and runs forward, and (Mr. Dove) follows her, bowing and bowing. And that makes her laugh again" (502). To the reader, this is already a very familiar scene.

While it is true that Anne is the stronger character, the one who controls the action, Reggie is the main character of the story. Seen through the eyes of the third-person point of view narrator, Reggie's thoughts and feelings are described for the reader, while only Anne's actions are revealed. Reggie is a shy person with little or no confidence in himself. A "widow's only son," Reggie has clearly been completely dominated by mom all his life. The closest thing Reggie has to siblings are mater's dogs, Biddy and Chinny; they both seem to be more in line than Reggie with mater's picture of what good children should be, obedient and faithful. This probably explains much of Reggie's inexplicable guilt feelings and his lack of confidence. Mansfield's biting descriptive scene of Reggie with Mater is very scary, for example, "the mater, with her scissors outspread to snap the head of a dead something or other, stopped at the sight of Reggie" (499). This quote seems to say it all about Reggie's relationship with mother. However, if the reader doesn't quite get it yet, Mansfield adds, "Snip. Off came a head. Reggie almost jumped" (499). It is not difficult, then, after reading this scene, to understand more about the strange relationship that Reggie has with Anne. He seems to be just as afraid of her as he is charmed by her. And she is in complete control of him.

The conflict concerns, of course, Reggie's proposal. Anne dreams of someone to come and take her away, to control her, and take care of her. At the same time, however, she revels in the control she has over Reggie and tells him that she is very happy around him. The conflict is only resolved when it seems to Anne that there is a chance that she does not have control over Reggie anymore. When it seems that he has given up his habit of following Anne around, she becomes angry. When he walks away from her, she seems to develop a new interest. At the ending of the story, we see what seems to be Anne's acceptance of Reggie's proposal and a return to their usual behavior when Anne calls, "Come back, Mr. Dove" (505).

"The Young Girl"

Mrs. Raddick, in "The Young Girl," her attractive 17-year-old daughter, and her young son Hennie are Londoners visiting the French Riviera. The seemingly bored young girl and her mother leave Hennie with a friend of Mrs. Raddick's, a French man, while they go gamble. The girl soon returns, too young to be admitted. She reluctantly accompanies her brother and the anonymous narrator to a cafe. Initially declaring lack of appetite, she nonchalantly echoes Hennie's orders of hot chocolate, pastries, and ice cream, then powders her nose. An elderly man, whom she either fails to notice or ignores, stares at her. Mrs. Raddick does not meet them at the promised time, and the young girl, close to tears, insists on waiting alone for her mother.

The moods in "The Young Girl" are of tension between immaturity, both psychological and physical, and of frustration, as illusion is confronted with bitter reality. The young girl is in a period of role transition between childhood and adulthood, struggling to establish her identity. That she is reaching physical maturity is evident in the narrator's perception of her as well as in the stares of other men, yet the Casino refuses to grant her the status of an adult due to her age. Age, however, is not necessarily an indication of maturity, for the young girl mothers the easily-flustered Mrs. Raddick. In contrast, her daughter feigns indifference to and disdain for both the Casino and the cafe, and acts as she believes a mature woman would—casually powdering her nose, disinterested in and mentally distant from all that goes on around her. Her illusions of maturity, represented in her performance, are undermined first in her rejection from the Casino, and then finally upon having to wait, humiliated, for her negligent mother once again. While men's appreciative stares invite her, her mother and the Casino reject her as a member of the adult world, and she no longer wishes to identify with Hennie's "childish" world. The result of her predicament is isolation.

This short story displays a Modernist scorn for materialism, as one becomes as a young child or even an animal when intoxicated with the smell of money at the Casino. Women are subordinated to the status of objects: the young girl is like the pastries in that her beauty is devoured by men in the story, and the role she practices is that of a stereotypical female. Childhood is no longer portrayed as carefree, but becomes characterized by anxiety, trauma, and repression.

"Life of Ma Parker"

Ma Parker, a grandmother, is the house-cleaner for a literary gentleman, who is both a slob and a snob. The gentleman asks several thoughtless questions about the death of her grandson, Lennie. As she cleans the apartment, she thinks about her life and Lennie. She recalls the horrible places she has lived and the death of her husband. Most of her 13 children are also dead. Ma Parker wonders what she has done to bring all this trouble to her life. She has nobody left and has nowhere to cry in private.

In true Modernist fashion, "Life of Ma Parker" is a very pessimistic story. Death and hopelessness are the primary images found in this story. The death of loved ones, particularly Lennie, provides a potent image. Life seems hopeless to Ma Parker because she has no one to turn to, and she has no place to cry without being disturbed. The literary gentleman is also hopeless because of his inability to take care of himself.

Mansfield also adds the somewhat positive idea of self-reliance. The literary gentleman can't take care of himself and must present a snobbish, eccentric attitude to the world. Ma Parker has learned how to take care of herself. The others, her husband and his sister, who could have helped her are either dead or incapacitated. She has had to deal with the deaths of her loved ones and continue on with her life. However, the death of her precious grandson, Lennie, is the straw that breaks the camel's back. She now sees the world as hopeless and therefore her self-reliance is shattered.

"Marriage A La Mode"

"Poor William" rides the train out of London weekly to visit for a day and a half his children, his wife Isabel, and unfortunately, her companions. Isabel and William's marriage has obviously changed, as Isabel has, for the worse. Isabel has been captured by the cool, elite, "jet set" type of social climbers who concern themselves with the new and intellectually posh people and modes of life. Instead of spending the short amount of time with her husband, Isabel plays with her so-called friends. On William's return to London the next day, he writes Isabel a love letter which she shockingly reads to her hangers-on for entertainment. Once she realizes the horror of this act, she becomes repulsed with herself, but of course, this moment of shame lasts no longer than the time which would be needed to peel the children's pineapple she took from William for herself.

This story illustrates the superficiality and potential harm of the artistic and celebrated becoming the victims of the social climbers Mansfield knew too well. These people and Isabel herself are running William and Isabel's marriage and family with their frivolity and shallowness. This shallow, superficial lifestyle focused on materialism is represented in a modernistic style by the often-mentioned color yellow, symbolizing the fake scene. A room in their new house is yellow and even one of the hangers-on acknowledges that there is "far too much yellow" (561) tinting their supper.

The reader pities William, especially when Isabel reads his love letter to her group, but he does not deserve much sympathy. He criticizes Isabel's ideas about their spoiled children playing with the foreign and "right" toys, but he does no better by buying their affection and forgiveness with either candy or fruit. Instead he should have kept his family in the city with him, therefore preventing his guilt. He is somewhat hypocritical when he reproves the snobbery of the social climbers because he, while on the first-class smoker, displays condescending disgust towards a poor girl and a black man as he pulls out of the train station. Moreover, he is the weak, inadequate man Mansfield detests because he does not rid his home of these leeches. Both he and Isabel have been changed by their new, stylish lifestyle and both should have "a la mode" wardrobes of yellow.

"The Voyage"

In her short story entitled "The Voyage," Mansfield relates the story of a young girl, Fenella, whose mother has very recently died. Fenella's father sends her to live with his parents, and most of the action of the story occurs on the voyage from Fenella's hometown to her grandparent's house. By entitling the story "The Voyage," Mansfield shows the double meaning of the word. The actual voyage which the two take is one on a boat, over rocky seas. The metaphorical voyage Mansfield writes about is Fenella's upcoming voyage through a somewhat turbulent adolescent life without the solid anchor of a mother.

Mansfield develops her story with a good amount of imagery relating to darkness. Everything in the story is dark: "It was very dark on the Old Wharf...all seemed carved out of solid darkness, her grandma bustled along in her crackling black ulster" (525). Since the story is told through the eyes of a very young girl who has just lost her mother, the inclusion of this darkness imagery is quite appropriate. In addition to both Fenella's and her grandmother's black attire, everything around Fenella is black. By using this imagery of darkness, Mansfield can easily show the uncertainty of Fenella's future. Since Fenella loses, in essence, both her mother and her father, her world would be black, with no cause for joy. Fenella loves her father dearly, and she expresses difficulty in understanding why she must be sent away to her grandmother's house. Her father gives her a brief kiss on the cheek and a shilling, both of which serve to only add to her confusion. However, once on the boat, Fenella's grandmother's attitude changes from one of somberness to one of cautious optimism. Fenella senses this change, and in turn, her mood brightens also.

The central conflict in "The Voyage" seems to rest between Fenella and her grandmother. A hint of resentment links the two characters. Fenella resents the substitution of her grandmother for her mother. The grandmother resents the burden of having to raise another child while nursing a sick husband. The one area which they share a common ground is the grandmother's umbrella, which is in the shape of a swan's head. They both realize that they must make the best of the situation they have been thrown into, and that they do, indeed, need each other. The young, graceful swan represents Fenella. Just as swans have no defenses, neither does Fenella. She has been thrown into a cold, cruel world with no one to protect her. The umbrella represents the grandmother, always there to protect Fenella from whatever dangers can be found.

It is interesting to note that Mansfield always has Fenella holding the umbrella. Just as the umbrella needs support in order to be effective, the grandmother depends on Fenella for support. Managing a household and nursing a sick husband are duties which require a great deal of energy. With Fenella around to help share the responsibility, the grandmother's life will be a little easier. The relationship between the two women is mutually beneficial. At the end of the story, Fenella is finally beginning to feel more secure. She finds a white, warm cat at her grandmother's house and a poem above her grandparents' bed. The poem deals with how time is fleeting, and the poem was written by her grandmother. The grandmother is given the opportunity to experience the "Golden Hour" of youth once again, and Fenella will be able to grow up with a mother figure, a woman who has a great deal of experience, and a woman who has lived most of the voyage Fenella is just beginning to undertake.

"Miss Brill"

Every Sunday Miss Brill emerges to watch the band. This is a particularly special Sunday because it is the beginning of the Season and she celebrates by wearing her fur which she has "rubbed the life back into" (549). Miss Brill entertains herself by watching and eavesdropping on other people from her "special" seat and contemplates how life is a play in which we all have a part, including herself. However, she is quickly drawn from her revelry when a young couple scorns her presence and makes fun of her "dear little" fox.

"Miss Brill" is a warning. The main character exists in a timeless world made of routines and fantasy. She has wasted her life by observing other people's lives instead of acting out a life of her own. As the lady has floated through the years, she has not acknowledged the fact that she has aged. Miss Brill does not realize that she fits into the group she so accurately describes.

...they were nearly always the same Sunday after Sunday, and—Miss Brill had often noticed—there was something funny about nearly all of them. They were odd, silent, nearly all old, and from the way they stared they looked as though they'd just come from dark little rooms or even—even cupboards! (551)

Instead of this reality, Miss Brill prefers to view herself as an actress performing a necessary role. "No doubt somebody would have noticed if she hadn't been there; she was a part of the performance after all" (552). By hiding behind her dreams, Miss Brill has taken the easy, passive path in life, a role which Mansfield abhorred.

Mansfield again asserts the wretchedness of mankind. The men of this story have no redeeming qualities. In the first encounter, Miss Brill listens testily as a man patronizes his wife. The next man she describes as "the Brute" because he pompously walks away from a lady as she is attempting to entertain him. The final male, who embodies all self-centered qualities, is the boy at the end of the story who pronounces her presence as unwelcome at this essential event in her life. The harsh disillusionment, which he imposes, forces her to face reality and return to what she now realizes is her "little dark room—her room like a cupboard" (553).

"Her First Ball"

KM's "Her First Ball" is a story about a young girl named Leila who has never experienced attending a ball. But one day, her cousins Laurie, Meg and Laura invite her to one. Prior to the ball, Leila tries very hard not to let her eagerness show, but despite her efforts, she is amazed by all of the preparations that she must make to attend this special event. On the night of the ball, Leila begs her mom to let her stay home, but her mom refuses. Therefore, Leila continues to prepare for her ball until her special night arrives. On the night of the ball, Leila finds herself enjoying and having a remarkable time, until she is approached by a fat man who not only asks her to dance, but also makes her realize that her first ball is not all that her cousins have led her to believe. Later, a damper is placed on Leila's special night when she is told by the fat man that "her first ball" is only the beginning of her last one.

The main character, Leila, is a young, innocent girl who experiences the thrill of her life when she attends her first ball. Leila grew up in the country where her nearest neighbor lived 15 miles away; therefore, when it comes to socializing, Leila has not had much experience. In addition, Leila is an only child who finds it very difficult to deal with the absence of a sibling. When she is around her cousins, sometimes she cannot help but cry, because she feels that she has been deprived of the opportunity to share the kind of closeness that brothers and sisters usually share. Leila also feels that she is not as responsible and mature as her cousins because they have experienced more than she. None of her cousins' friends can believe that a girl Leila's age has never attended a ball. Hence, Leila is chaperoned by her cousins throughout the night, and she is often referred to as their "country cousin."

The conflict in the story takes place on the night of Leila's ball. Uncertain whether or not anyone will ask her to dance, Leila is surprised when she is approached by a fat, older man who asks her to dance. At this ball, only the young people dance, and Leila is confused as to why this man is not seated on stage with the rest of the elderly people. However, Leila does not try to embarrass this man but instead commends him on his ability to be able to keep up with the teen-age, fast-paced dances. As the band continues to play and Leila and her partner continue to dance, the fat man exposes Leila to an inevitable truth. He makes her cognizant of the fact that she will not always look as beautiful as she does on this night. He also tells her that someday the flesh from her beautiful arms will droop, and age will have taken its toll on her. He continues by telling Leila that before she knows it, she will be sitting on stage with the rest of the elderly people, and instead of her admiring the ball floor, she will be threatened by it with the fear that she could possibly fall.

After Leila digests all that her partner has told her, she's not so sure that her evening is really special. In the middle of a song, Leila decides that she no longer wants to dance. She suddenly realizes that her happiness is not going to last forever, and the music that once fascinated her has now sent her into a depression. When her partner sees the effect that this information has taken on Leila, he tries to revive her spirits by telling her that he was only kidding; to Leila this is no joke. In the meantime, Leila tries to find her cousins so she can go home. In a very short time, a night that was supposed to be so special had suddenly turned into one of despair.

"The Singing Lesson"

"The Singing Lesson" begins with the wicked Miss Meadows making her way through the school's hollow corridors in route to the music hall to fulfill her role as music director. Any encounter Miss Meadows meets on the way is warded off by her dagger-like stare and cold remarks. The air of happiness in the music hall is totally admonished upon her entry. The songs that are sung are filled with despair, driving the young girls to tears. "Every note was a sigh, a sob, a groan of awful mournfulness" (493). Mansfield enters Miss Meadows sporadic thoughts into the story, clueing the reader into the reason for her grief. Miss Meadows' fiance, Basil, has broken their engagement saying that the thought of commitment fills him with "nothing but disgust" (494). Miss Meadows is summoned to the school office and receives a telegram. To her relief it is from Basil, informing her that he has changed his mind. The wedding is on. Miss Meadows is transformed into a joyous woman, bursting with happiness.

Mansfield uses irony as the key to her meaning. Once again the female character is completely dependent upon the male. Like a verse in the song, Mansfield portrays Miss Meadows like a fish wriggling on the end of a line. Her fiance is her source of life, her water. Without him, her madness is frightening. She suffocates herself internally at the thought of terminating the relationship. On the surface this seems to be the perfect story-book ending. Miss Meadows is drunk from the naivete of her love for Basil. Though she is satisfied and does not question his sudden decision, Mansfield leads the reader to believe that the opposite is true.

Happiness is excluded from the story. The dull feeling of depression that the reader feels at the end is, indeed, the emotion that Mansfield seems to be striving for. As mournful as it begins, so does it end, despite Miss Meadows' facade of happiness. The reader can see that Miss Meadows is in for more regret than she originally felt, and would be better off to suffer the initial hurt than to be bound to Basil forever. The plot goes back to the old cliche, if it's too good to be true, it's usually not true. Either Miss Meadows is entering into a marriage with a maniac, or the dagger-like stares she feels now will one day be driven to the point of actual knives, driven by his inhuman manipulation. The violent tendency that Miss Meadows feels now will in time be much worse than making young girls sing mournful songs. The reader is conscious of the mistake Miss Meadows is about to make. She obviously has no self-esteem since Mansfield tells us that she does not care how much Basil loves her. Just that he cares a little is all that Miss Meadows wants. The name Miss Meadows is symbolic of its literal meaning. A meadow is an open field that people love to trample upon. There you have it, the story seems to be saying.

"The Stranger"

"The Stranger," like Mansfield's "The Escape," explores the relationship between a husband and wife, and the ironic twists and turns inherent in such a relationship. Mansfield often employs a very cynical tone in her stories about marriage because she views that institution as repressive and conventional. The Hammonds' marriage is a perfect example of this idea. The story is set on the day that Mrs. Hammond returns from a ten-month's journey overseas to visit her married daughter in Europe. Although they have been married quite some time, Mr. Hammond is still quite enamored with his wife, which is revealed in his impatience on the dock because the boat is delayed in docking, and in his shaking hands and pounding heart. He has always secretly feared that his wife does not love him as much as he loves her, and when he greets her on the boat, he is too eager to get her away from a place in which he has had no share in her life to the hotel room where they can supposedly be alone together. Mr. Hammond is desperate to reclaim his wife, to reaffirm his love for her, but what happens in that room is not a reaffirmation, but a confirmation of Mr. Hammond's worst fears. His wife has not missed him at all, and she never really loved him enough to take him into her arms, as she did the dying man on the boat.

The main character of "The Stranger" is Mr. John Hammond, a successful businessman probably in his late forties or early fifties. The picture of the perfect Edwardian gentleman, Mr. Hammond is well-dressed in a grey overcoat, grey silk scarf, gloves, and a hat. His personality, while he is kind and well meaning, is as colorless as his attire. He is obsessed with his wife to the detriment of his mental ability. Like the husband in Kate Chopin's "The Story of an Hour," Mr. Hammond's love for his wife is expressed in his desire "to make Janey so much a part of him that there wasn't any of her to escape" (455). His love is repressive and overbearing, but he cannot see what it is doing to his wife or himself. He wants from her what she seems to be afraid to give, for fear that one small crack in her defenses will allow him to overcome her totally. He is characterized by Mansfield as "something between the sheep-dog and the shepherd" (446), always trying gently to drive his wife in the direction he wishes her to go, and reacting with surprise when she seems to have a mind of her own. Mr. Hammond is a conservative man who enjoys the simple pleasures of life, such as a comfortable routine and a wife who dotes on his every word. He is deathly afraid of any change in his relationship with his wife, and this partly accounts for his apprehension at her return. He also has hopes that her prolonged absence might have increased his wife's affection for him, but the news that she helped a dying man by holding him in her arms ends any such idea. Mr. Hammond is devastated by the thought of his wife's giving too freely to a stranger what she has denied him for so many years.

The main conflict in "The Stranger" is between Mr. Hammond's notion of a closed-off, possessive kind of love, and Mrs. Hammond's need to experience other emotions besides her husband's love. Mr. Hammond refuses to see his wife as she really is, but sets her up to be a perfect dream woman who will never change. One of his first thoughts as he greets Janey on the boat is, "She was just the same. Not a day changed. Just as he'd always known her" (450). If he can know his wife, down to the smallest details of her day, Hammond feels that he can truly possess her, and lose his gnawing fear of her flying away. Hammond hates to have her attention shifted away from him for a moment, yet she seems to be an outgoing, personable woman, to judge from the reaction of her shipmates at the end of her journey. Mrs. Hammond does not share her husband's obsessive love. She cares for him deeply, but the idea of change does not scare her as much as her husband. She has obviously enjoyed herself during her travels, and her remarks to Mr. Hammond are telling. "You've had your beard beautifully trimmed, and you look—younger, I think, and decidedly thinner! Bachelor life agrees with you" (452).

Her words are a vain attempt to hide the truth from herself, however, because when they return to the hotel, one look at John's dressing table is enough to tell her that he has not and probably never will change. The story she tells her husband of the dying man is not meant to hurt him, but the serious lack of communication between the couple leads to Mr. Hammond's vehement reaction. She will never understand the deep well of need he has inside him, and he will never know why she is incapable of giving him the kind of love he desires. The title of the story refers to the ironic ending—the stranger Mrs. Hammond has become, and the stranger who has come between them forever.

"Bank Holiday"

Through a brief descriptive vignette, KM examines a frivolous day at a carnival. An omniscient narrator scans the setting of a warm spring day's fair to reveal that the people visiting the fair live boring, pointless lives. The story's title implies that these working-class fairgoers seek a respite from the tedium of their jobs. The fair provides that respite, and is a goal in itself, perhaps even the reason for existence for most of the people.

Mansfield uses a panoramic narrative method to convey the fair's atmosphere: she first describes particular individuals, revealing their simple yet hollow pleasures, activities that indeed bore a few of them; then she increases the breadth of her picture, putting the individual into a large collective swarm that moves together and has the same destination—uncertainty. Yet at the narrative's center appear the hucksters, tramps who draw the people into crowds and prey on empty lives, but ironically provide those lives with temporary variety.

While Mansfield offers no specific protagonist, she does single out individuals. She emphasizes the amateur musicians first, as they earnestly but routinely play their instruments with expressions that are, "unsmiling, not serious"—only jaded (436). Through the narrator, the reader overhears bits of conversation, all of it inconsequential and important only to the speakers. After she singles out a few individuals, Mansfield views them as a mass, "moving slowly up the hill" (437) to where the hucksters wait to scavenge the crowd. As the salesmen advertise their wares, the people step gaily into spending frenzies, eager to stroke their own vanities and the vanities of their loved ones. Feathers are the most popular items, but a "shrivelled, ageless Italian" woman's caged "love birds" attract interest as they "tell you your future" (438). The fortune-telling woman is reaping the benefits of a crowd which, like all crowds of all sizes, unconsciously fears the uncertainty of fate, yet marches toward it in time as they move en masse up the hill.

Thus Mansfield offers a metaphor for life itself. But in her description, working-class people are not struggling against the hucksters and are not fighting each other; they exist in a strange harmony, a unity as they move through the spring warmth toward uncertain ends. They push on as if denying the proximity of their deaths, as if accustomed to uncertainty and ignorance. Their oblivion is a defense against the anxiety of fate, and their happiness—however empty—is their sustenance. Mansfield makes this conflict with fate clearest at the end, where the crowd climbs up the hill "as though (being) pushed by something, far below, and by the sun, far ahead of them" (439). Perhaps that vague "something" is the will to live, an instinct evident from birth; and perhaps the sun is faith, or a tenuous hope that the uncertain fate will ultimately have reward. For now, the crowd moves on despite the daunting question the narrator asks on their behalf: "what?" (439).

"An Ideal Family"

"An Ideal Family" focuses on the fragmented, fading life of elderly Mr. Neave, a successful businessman, and a figure of authority. Mansfield shows him as a victim of his age, his society's values, and his own family. KM examines the tragedy of a man who has outlived his own authority. He is the head of "an ideal family," shown at the moment of his failing strength, dressing for dinner with his family but shifted to the sidelines by his preoccupied wife and self-indulgent children. He created his family's bounty, enjoyed manifestly by them in their home. He made their "ideal" and now finds himself alienated and estranged from the world he has created.

Mr. Neave now spends his day perpetually moving between fading life and a rapidly approaching death. He lives in the illusory world between dreams and reality; he is anesthetized by the neglect he has fallen into. He goes in and out of extended reveries, searching for familiar faces, for acceptance, for kindness. But, he always awakens to the harsh reality of a family who no longer cares who he is, nor what he had accomplished for them. His family is pushing him out of the business he spent his whole life building for them—"Why will you be so unreasonable, father? There's absolutely no need for you to go to the office.... You could take up some hobby" (507). He is being pushed aside in his own home—"Old Mr. Neave, forgotten, sank into the broad lap of his chair, and dozing, heard them as though he dreamed" (510). His family simply leaves his welfare up to his manservant, Charles. Never are they concerned with his thoughts or feelings. They only shuffle him off to be seen to, saying—"Dress him up, Charles!" Consequently, Mr. Neave begins to see himself as a "withered ancient man climbing up endless flights of stairs" (510). He has nothing to live for, and is constantly moving toward oblivion. Yet, he always recalls being told that he has "an ideal family." And, with sad and tormenting irony, the falseness of this empty phrase haunts him. He questions the ideality of a family that leaves him forever "all alone, climbing up and down" (511) a staircase leading nowhere.

"The Lady's Maid"

In form, Mansfield's story "The Lady's Maid" is a dramatic monologue, in which Ellen, the lady's maid, tells her life story along with details of her relationship with her mistress to an unnamed listener. The listener does speak seven words at the story's opening before Ellen begins (*"Eleven o'clock. A knock at the door..."*) (450), but the two sentences are italicized to set them off from the maid's speech. Even though the listener is not named, it is clear that she is a woman and a guest in the house, for the maid addresses her as "madam." The maid seems talkative and seldom at a loss for words, but the female listener encourages Ellen to tell her story by asking questions and commenting. Her questions and comments are unstated yet are represented by an ellipsis at the beginning of paragraphs in which the lady's maid responds directly to what the listener has said. It is, however, relatively easy to construct what the listener says by examining Ellen's responses.

Let's examine how the listener encourages the maid to tell her story. 1) The house guest comments on the cup of tea Ellen brings her, perhaps saying simply, "Thank you." The maid reveals that her lady always has tea before retiring, after she has said her prayers. As Ellen tucked in her mistress tonight, she was reminded of the lady's dead mother. 2) The listener asks about the funeral preparations; "Did you take care of the arrangements?" (459). Yes, the maid says; she even arranged the dead woman's hair, "all in dainty curls," and put a bunch of purple pansies near her head. Tonight with her lady only the flowers were missing from the picture. 3) "Did her disease affect her greatly," asks the guest, who seems to know that it had been a form of insanity. "Only the last year, madam." Ellen is quick to add that the woman was "never dangerous" but only "couldn't keep still" (459). She believed that she'd lost something and entreated the maid to find it for her. 4) The next question seems to be about the insane woman's condition: "Did she recover before her death?" No, the listener learns from the maid, the lady's mother never recovered before dying of a stroke, and her final words were " 'Look in— the—Look—in—' " (459). 5) The house guest seems to commiserate with the servant girl and perhaps says, "It must be a difficult life for you." Since Ellen's own mother has died of consumption, however, the maid has no choice but to stay in service. "I've got nobody but my lady" (459). For a time as a child she lived with her grandfather who ran a hairdressing salon. 6) Here the listener interjects a "Yes?" to keep the maid talking. Ellen goes on with a story about how one day she cut off her hair and her grandfather was so furious that her burned her fingers in the curling irons. 7) Interested in the grandfather's motives, "madam" most likely asks, "Why did he do that?" It seems the old man was extremely proud of Ellen's hair and often arranged it, giving the little girl a penny to hold as he did, though always taking the coin back when he was finished. After being burned, the girl ran away. 8) The guest, who seems more concerned about the grandfather's loss than the little girl's burnt fingers, wonders, "Did he ever get over it?" The maid replies that he "never got over it" and "couldn't eat" (460), so that in the end she was sent to live with her aunt, a tiny, crippled upholstress, through whom she met her lady.

9) "You must have been very young" may be the next comment. The listener learns that Ellen was 13 when she went into service. "And I don't remember ever feeling—well—a child" (460). But a moment later she recalls feeling like a child once when she escorted her lady's two nieces to a local fair so they could ride the donkeys. The nieces don't ride, but Ellen wanted to ride very much. 10) The guest asks the maid, "Why didn't you ride?" "I couldn't," she replies, for she was in uniform and had a responsibility to her "young ladies." All that day, however, Ellen thought about the donkey ride. 11) Here the listener wants to know if the lady's maid ever considers leaving her employer, perhaps asking, "Do you ever think of marrying?" (462). The servant tells her that at one time she was engaged to a florist, Harry, but gave up the idea on the day they were to pick out their furniture because her lady acted strange—picking up her own handkerchief, making the same gesture as her dead mother. So when Harry arrived Ellen returned his letters, ring, and brooch, and she closed the door in his face. 12) The house guest says nothing, but the striking clock moves the maid to end her story. She apologizes for keeping the guest awake and admits her dependence on her lady. 13) In this ellipsis the listener remains quiet as if the momentum of the maid's speech is enough to lead Ellen on to consider what she

would do if anything were to happen to her mistress. But she concludes, "Thinking won't help" (463).

What, then, does the lady's maid reveal about herself under the house guest's questioning? The most obvious aspect of her life story is that Ellen—orphaned, abused by her grandfather, sent to live with her crippled aunt, and pressed into service at age 13—has been denied a childhood. She admits as much. "And I don't remember ever feeling—well—a child, as you might say" (460). The closest she came to being a girl was when, at her grandfather's hairdressing shop, she played with her doll under the table. Then the assistants were "ever so kind" to her. That relatively happy time ended, however, when her grandfather burned her fingers, scarring her for life, because she had cut her hair. Although seemingly stoic about her lot, Ellen has, on at least one occasion, wished to act like a girl. She wanted ever so much to ride the donkeys at a local fair, but her duties prevented her. And yet the desire was so strong that the maid contrived a way to express her wish—she acted as though she were sleeping and dreaming before exclaiming, " 'I do want a donkey-ride!' " (461). Relating the episode to the listener, Ellen derives her action as what a "silly child" would do. And at the story's end, engaged in what she considers childish behavior—thinking about the future—the maid again criticizes herself as a "silly girl."

Forced to accept adult responsibilities from an earlier age, the lady's maid seems to view childhood as an age of silliness, a time of her life she has lost though lost with few regrets. Mansfield underscores the theme of Ellen's lost childhood in the character of the lady's mad mother who looked at the maid "just like a child" and cried, " 'I've lost it.' " What has the old woman lost but her childhood? At death she seems on the verge of telling Ellen where to look, and the ambiguity of the passage suggests the dying woman might have given the maid a clue to finding what's been lost. Despite her unhappy life, the maid tells her story dispassionately and without self-pity as though she has never expected anything more. True, she has not been mistreated by her lady (compare the servant-girl in another Mansfield story, "The Child-Who-Was-Tired"), but Ellen, throughout her life, has been controlled by those around her. Her grandfather gave her a penny to hold while he dressed her hair, though when finished he retrieved the coin. On one hand her mistress tells the maid every night, " 'Sleep sound and wake early!' " (459), a blessing Ellen says she cannot live without, while on the other, the lady manipulated her servant's feelings in such a way that Ellen broke off her engagement to the florist. The relationship between lady and maid resembles that of an overbearing mother and a child too dependent on her. Has her lady become a surrogate mother to Ellen? If that is the case, then the story seems to hinge upon a paradox. Ellen has never been allowed to be a child in any conventional sense, and yet at an age when she should be an adult, she is locked into playing a child's role opposite her lady. Never a child yet always a child. That is the impression Mansfield creates in the character of the lady's maid.

Chapter Six
Stories from the Posthumous Collection
The Dove's Nest and Other Stories (1923)

Before her death in 1923, KM planned to include six stories about New Zealand and three about London in her fourth volume. But because of the severity of her illness, she was only able to write four stories; all were about New Zealand. Among these stories were "The Doll's House" and "The Fly." Even though both are regarded as two of her most outstanding achievements, "The Fly" is considered to be Mansfield's last great story. In this story Mansfield expresses some hateful feelings towards her father; most of the story is based on circumstances that took place between her and her father. Also included in this volume is "A Married Man's Story" which was written shortly after Mansfield married Murry. During the time in which it was written, Mansfield and Murry were having major marriage problems. Especially the never-finished stories from this set have the sound of a sociopath writing. These incomplete stories are vividly gothic and established at a preconscious level.

The Dove's Nest and Other Stories was the first posthumous volume put together by J.M. Murry. Published in 1923, it contains only one complete story originally planned by KM, "The Doll's House," originally titled "At Karori," although the title of the collection is the one she had planned to use. Of the other six works planned, fragments remain of "Weak Heart," "Honesty," "Second Violin," "Six Years After," and "Widowed." There remains no trace of the three other stories. It is possible to determine from Mansfield's plan and the remaining fragments that she was continuing the themes from her earlier collections, such as her New Zealand childhood, death, and women on their own. Yet she also planned to write longer works, such as the unfinished "The Dove's Nest" and the never seen "Lives Like Logs of Driftwood."

Murry wrote a long introduction to *The Dove's Nest* in which he announced his intention to publish a collection of KM's earlier works, and explained why he chose certain works to be included in this collection. He includes all stories completed between October 1921 and June 1922, which would probably have been included had Mansfield lived, and leads off the collection with "The Doll's House," another story set in New Zealand featuring the same family in "Prelude" and "At the Bay." Murry also explains through excerpts from KM's journal the clarity she was trying to find in her writing. He is already beginning his campaign to establish KM as one of the preeminent writers of her age. He calls her talent "among the rarest of her generation," and excuses his inclusion of her unfinished stories by saying, "it has seemed to me that there is not a scrap of her writing—not even the tiniest fragment—during this final period which does not bear the visible impress of her exquisite individuality and her creative power" (Murry 383).

"The Doll's House"

"When dear old Mrs. Hay went back to town after staying with the Burnells she sent the children a doll's house" (570). The house stood in the Burnell's courtyard, reeking of paint, oily green with a yellow front door and porch and two red and white chimneys. Thus begins "The Doll's House." The Burnell children, Isabel, Lottie, and Kezia, were overwhelmed. The most impressive parts were, as always with toys, the parts that were real and not simply pretend. Kezia seemed to look for a special kind of realness in the house; she was looking for something friendly that belonged. She spotted a tiny oil lamp on the dining-room table. It was at home in the doll's house, unlike the dolls who sprawled out stiff and were rather too large. Isabel got to brag about the doll's house the next day at school because she was oldest and bossy, but Kezia got in a couple of words about the wonderful lamp. The girls at school wanted so to be Isabel's friend that day, because Isabel was also the one to pick who would get to come and see the doll's house first. The little girls were to come each day in pairs to see the doll's house; only into the courtyard, of course, so they wouldn't disturb the grown-ups.

The day came when all the little girls at school had seen the doll's house except the Kelveys, and no one expected them to be asked. Lil and Else Kelvey were the daughters of a washerwoman. They came to school dressed in scraps, and no one knew where their father was—probably in prison. The Kelveys wouldn't have even been in the same school with children like the Burnells if it hadn't been the only school in the neighborhood. Still, the teacher knew to treat the Kelveys a little differently from her other pupils, and the other little girls never played with the Kelveys. That day when everyone had seen the doll's house but the Kelveys, the lunchtime conversation lagged, so the nice children made some fun out of taunting the common little Kelvey girls. It was exhilarating! "The little girls rushed away in a body, deeply, deeply excited, wild with joy" (575). Everyone knew how to treat the Kelveys except Kezia. That afternoon Kezia saw the Kelveys walking home from school, and she let them see the doll's house. They even got to see the lamp before Kezia's Aunt Beryl saw them in the courtyard and chased the Kelveys away. It was appalling, and the Burnells had company, too. Beryl's afternoon had been awful. "A letter had come from Willie Brent, a terrifying, threatening letter, saying if she did not meet him that night in Pulman's Bush, he'd come to the front door and ask the reason why! But now that she had frightened those little rats of Kelveys and given Kezia a good scolding, her heart felt lighter. That ghastly pressure was gone. She went back to the house humming" (577).

Mansfield draws some very disturbing comparisons in this story. She delivers one prickling point after another; the reader is caught in the parallel between the teacher's subtle smiles and the little girls' outright exclusion of the Kelveys. Once again Mansfield demands an active reader, one who will see the parallel between the schoolgirls' glee and Beryl's humming when both have abused the Kelveys. KM came from a wealthy family, and she was uncomfortable with this wealth. She knew how class distinctions work; the difference between adults' and children's prejudices is that adult prejudice is refined to an art form.

When the reader connects with the emotions of this story, that is the moment when Mansfield takes control. She can be cutting in her manipulation of her reader, but this story has a brightening at the end, which is unusual for Mansfield. The brightness is Else's "rare smile" as she says, " 'I seen the little lamp' " (577). Or, perhaps the unbitter sadness of the pathetic Kelveys makes Else's smile more upsetting than brightening.

"Honeymoon"

As evidenced in other stories, Mansfield's "Honeymoon" seems, at first, light-hearted and comical. However, as this short story unfolds, it is clearly characterized by dejection and depression. As with some of her other stories, the reader must begin with characters and settings Mansfield presumed to be familiar. So it is with George and his bride, Fanny, who are honeymooning on the Riviera. They are surrounded by lobed leaf "plane trees" (sycamores and buttonwoods), heliotropes, and the beautiful, enchanting Mediterranean Sea. As George and Fanny emerge from the "lace shop," he summons a horse-powered "cab," and off they go, in high spirits, to a hotel restaurant, where they later enjoy tea and chocolate eclairs. En route to this restaurant by-the-sea, Fanny and George observe the sights: the small streets, the smell of lemon and coffee, the women carrying water pots, the people bathing in the Mediterranean, and the exquisite villa, which dazzles the young people.

Upon arrival at the restaurant, Fanny and George are greeted by waiters and seated on the terrace. George asserts himself, rather arrogantly, as the manager simply tries to do his job, which, above all, is to please his customers. As they converse, Fanny, who is quite serious, rattles on about couples knowing each other and understanding each other. George reassures her, laughingly, that he does know "his Fanny...perfectly" (582). While sipping tea, they were surprised when a band suddenly began to play. As Fanny observes other guests, she is more intrigued by the band members, especially an "old man with white hair," who later sings with the band. Fanny, feeling overwhelmed by visible signs of suffering in the Spanish singer's voice and appearance, and George, feeling immersed in the newness of his relationship with Fanny, retreat to the hotel.

Fanny and George are described by the narrator as being "fat, good-natured, and smiling" (578). Fanny, exuding warmth and love, feels uncomfortable, occasionally, with George's actions. For instance, she was bothered at the way he "summoned cabs," but since the drivers were not upset, she quickly accepted his way of doing things. In fact, she articulates that George has a way of making things "sound so very nice" (579). A short time later, Fanny's tolerance is tested as George is disagreeable with *all* the waiter's suggestions, while Fanny sits there, appearing to be calm, "praying the manager would go" (580).

Fanny's favorite word while honeymooning is "extraordinary." There is subtle beauty in this clue, for it reveals that she is a sensitive, humble human being, who does not mind acknowledging that this honeymoon is definitely beyond what is usual, ordinary, and customary in her life. Fanny loves George so much that she vows never to interfere with her "husband's pleasure," and she exhibits her patience and tolerance of his irascible behavior by never disagreeing with him, especially at the restaurant. George loves Fanny, too; however, he lacks her sensitivity. He prefers to be seen as a confident man, fully accustomed to the ways of the world.

The conflict in "Honeymoon" is two-fold. Fanny is desirous of a serious answer when she confronts George—"Do you feel that you really know me?" (582). This represents the first sign of an internal struggle. For two people to know and to understand each other is very important to Fanny. She struggles internally with her feelings about the "old man...white hair" (582). As Fanny closely observes him, she sees suffering; she sees pain. As she listens to him sing, she hears in his voice a plea, a cry for help. Through empathy, Fanny knows that "there are people like this" (583). Her empathy takes on a global perspective.

As she looks at the beautiful sea, the brightness of the sky and considers her happiness and George's happiness, she wonders is it "right to be so happy," while others grow old and suffer. Growing old is inevitable; suffering is not. Fanny's ultimate hope is for human understanding. In a pensive mood, Fanny turns to George; she realizes that he does not share her sentiments. George, self-satisfied, is not empathic. He is too self-centered to consider expanding his horizon, for he already feels that his knowledge is superior. George is immersed in celebrating what he sees as a new beginning. To George, the old, Spanish singer represents the end—death; Fanny, on the other hand, represents a new beginning—life. George believes that it is "...terrific...at the beginning of everything...he and Fanny" (581). For different reasons, the couple escapes the depression and gloom brought on by the singer; the honeymooners retire to their hotel.

"A Cup of Tea"

Mansfield's "A Cup of Tea" is a sarcastic, and above all ironic story about a rich, highly fashionable, young girl named Rosemary Fell, who finds that being a "Good Samaritan" isn't always the smart thing to be. One day while shopping, Rosemary is accosted by a young girl who asks her for the price of a cup of tea. Instead of obliging the young girl's simple request, Rosemary decides to complicate the matter by taking the girl home with her. When they arrive at Rosemary's house, the young girl is afraid that Rosemary is going to call the police. When Rosemary assures her that she will not, and gains the young girl's confidence, she tells Rosemary to address her as Miss Smith. Later Phillip, Rosemary's husband, arrives home. Thinking that her husband will admire her good deed, Rosemary is furious when she finds that her husband admires Miss Smith more than Rosemary's good deed.

The main character, Rosemary Fell, is a brilliant, very modern, extremely stylish young woman who can be described as beautiful; however, pretty might be a more appropriate word. In her spare time, which is quite often, Rosemary enjoys shopping and buying expensive materials. Whenever she goes in stores, her selections always come from the finest qualities. Her favorite store is a little antique shop located in Paris. The man who keeps the shop always reserves his unique items for Rosemary because he not only has a crush on her, but he also knows that his special items will be in good hands. In the stores, Rosemary is what one might call a "preferred customer." Even though Rosemary spends most of her time shopping, she also enjoys reading and hosting fabulous parties. How does she afford such a glamourous life style? The answer is simple. Rosemary is married, and has been for two years, to a man who is very rich. Together they have a son named Michael, and whenever Rosemary is not tending to the family, she spends most of her time cruising the streets and looking for adventure.

The conflict arises in the story the day, while on one of her shopping ventures, Rosemary meets a thin, young girl on the streets of Paris. While thinking how hot it is, Rosemary decides to go home to get a cup of tea. While thinking this, she is approached by this young girl who is not much older than Rosemary. In the midst of the young girl's trembling, she asks Rosemary if she can have the price of a cup of tea; Rosemary is astonished, yet thrilled. Helping this young girl seems so exciting to her; therefore, she decides to take the girl home with her. Upon their arrival, the young girl is surprised by Rosemary's kindness; the young girl assumes that Rosemary is going to call the police. When Rosemary assures her that she will not, the young girl feels relieved. Thereafter, Rosemary not only gives the young girl all the tea she can drink, but also gives her all the food she is able to devour. After dinner, Phillip comes home; he questions the identity of the young girl. Rosemary introduces her as Miss Smith. Then Rosemary explains to him that the girl is someone she picked up off the streets; Phillip is not too pleased about the situation. He tries to make Rosemary understand that they cannot keep the girl, and in the process, he inadvertently mentions Miss Smith's beauty; he comments that she is adorable. Instantaneously going from a sympathetic young woman to a very irate wife, Rosemary realizes that she must ask Miss Smith to leave. It is quite obvious that Rosemary's jealousy overrides her sympathy. However, being a woman true to her word, Rosemary gives Miss Smith two pounds to take care of her necessities. Later when Phillip questions Miss Smith's whereabouts, Rosemary simply says "Miss Smith had to leave" (591).

"Taking the Veil"

This Mansfield story is a satirical portrait of a young woman mired in a syrupy mess of melodrama. If Mansfield were writing in our time, she might have depicted the main character, 18-year-old Edna, as reading romance novels, those with cover illustrations featuring ripped bodices and bare-chested he-men, and keeping up with the afternoon soaps. Poor Edna. Whether someone else's fantasies—the stage-play—or her own—her daydreams in the convent garden—she is too easily moved by what strikes the readers, and Mansfield, as sentimental nonsense. At the stage-play, when the hero goes blind ("Terrible moment!"), Edna cries buckets of tears, so many that she must borrow her fiance's handkerchief for her own has become tear-soaked. Her fiance,

Jimmy, remains dry-eyed during the histrionic performance, passing her chocolate-almonds and encouraging her to buck up. She seems to find his composure cold-hearted, and the next day contrives a fantasy in which she dies and Jimmy mourns by her graveside. "The tears are running down his face; he is crying *now*"(596). Edna's fantasy arises from what she sees as her dilemma: having fallen head over heels in love with the actor playing the blind hero, she must "decide somehow what was to be done now" (594). Of course, she must break her engagement with Jimmy. "But she,—what did the future hold for her?" (594). As Edna sits in the convent's garden the day after the stage-play, having already in her imagination broken off the engagement, a nun's voice reaches her ear, and in "that moment the future was revealed" (594). She will become a nun.

However, taking the veil proves to be only the starting point for her daydream, and readers chuckle as she borrows the cliches of melodrama to embroider on her future life. Edna ships to the actor her last photo in a box of white roses and sends to broken-hearted Jimmy a lock of her shorn hair. On an icy winter night, Edna, or Sister Angela as she will be known, rescues "some stray animal" from the garden, but her kindness is rewarded with a fever and an early death. Although by all logic, being dead, she shouldn't be able to witness the scene unless as an angel, Edna watches her parents and fiance shedding tears at her grave. "The world is cruel, terribly cruel" as she would say, though readers may be saying, "How trite, how incredibly trite." Mansfield treats us to one last fantasy of this melodramatic woman—Edna is reunited with Jimmy to have babies and plant roses.

Her propensity to view the world in the pale moonlight of melodrama is Edna's most obvious characteristic, but there are other facets of her personality although none which endears the young woman to her creator or readers. Edna seems self-centered, holds an exalted opinion of herself, and exaggerates as naturally as most people breathe. Her belief that no one suffers as she does illustrates Edna's self-centeredness. "Nobody was (unhappy), decided Edna, except herself." And in her fantasy when friends try to prevent her from entering the convent, she wonders why they "add to her suffering like this?" It's as if human emotions never existed before she experienced them, an opinion often held by adolescents. The solar system in this character's eyes follows an Edna-centric model: the sun and planets revolve around her; family members and friends visit from deep space as meteors, existing only as they pass through her orbit. Edna would follow the actor "without giving another thought to Jimmy or her father and mother or her happy home and countless friends again..." (593). As a result of her self-absorption, Edna has an elevated image of herself. In her fantasy Edna becomes not a mere nun but a saint, whereas the religious name she adopts, Sister Angela, suggests that Edna aspires to sit among the heavenly host. "She possesses a positive self-image," today's psycho-babblers would claim, which is all well and good, but in Edna's case it seems self-inflation, a species of exaggeration. In fact, she litters her speech and thought with exaggerations. The descriptions of Edna's feelings can best be summed up in the phrase "oh, the most," for she expresses her emotions in the superlative. Love, for example, is "the most dreadful sensation of hopeless misery, despair, agony and wretchedness" (593). As a form of stretching the truth, "never" also crops up frequently as Edna imagines how the players in her fantasies will act. Jimmy "would never get over" their breakup, yet when he pleads in her imagination for Edna to change her mind, she vows, " 'I will never change'."

It seems apparent that Mansfield created Edna to be the butt of her satire, a character held up to ridicule. As the writer intended, Edna's actions and fantasies in themselves reveal an adolescent of ridiculously melodramatic nature, yet at the same time Mansfield paints her creation in such an unfavorable light that readers readily grasp her own feelings toward the character. With one hand Mansfield beckons Edna from her imagination, while in the other she holds a lemon meringue pie. And Edna, poor Edna, takes it in the face. At the stage-play when she falls in love with the actor, Edna "drew her hand away from Jimmy's, leaned back and shut the chocolate box for ever" (592). To fall out of love with one's fiance and then become infatuated with an actor could be the material of both tragedy and romance, but in this story the detail of the chocolate almonds works to underscore the silliness of the infatuation. In a similar way, Edna's vagueness about the type of animal she will rescue after taking the veil ("a kitten or a lamb or—well, whatever little animal might be there") leaves her with pie on her nun's habit. Mansfield also uses irony to make clear her amused feelings toward her character. "It is not easy to look tragic at eighteen" (592), she writes before describing the unhappy but healthy young woman. And as though distinguishing between kinds of love, that is between Edna's love and everyone else's in the world, the writer employs dashes: "But—fallen—in—love..." Further irony lies in the fact that Edna uses that line when she falls *out* of love with Jimmy and later when she falls back *in* love with him. In love with her fiance again, Edna "had never imagined any feeling like it before" (593), apparently forgetting that four pages earlier she made the same claim for what she felt for the actor. Thus, with irony and literary slapstick, Mansfield satirizes her creation in "Taking the Veil," and leaves readers with the unfavorable impression that Edna is just a silly daydreamer mired in a mess of melodrama.

"The Fly"

In her short story entitled "The Fly," KM examines the lives of two central characters, old Mr. Woodifield and his boss. Mr. Woodifield worked for several years until he suffered a stroke. The only time his wife and daughters let him out of his house is on Tuesdays, the days which he visited his old work place. On this particular Tuesday, however, the visit is somewhat different. To appease the old man, the boss listens to the old man talk, but he never really hears what the old man is saying. The moment at which he begins to listen is when the old man says that his daughters recently visited a cemetery in Belgium, the cemetery which held the corpses of the sons of both men. Mr. Woodifield said, "The girls were in Belgium last week having a look at poor Reggie's grave, and they happened to come across your boy's. They're quite near each other, it seems" (599). This statement caused a great deal of grief and anguish to come flooding back to the boss. He then dismissed Mr. Woodifield, and decided to spend some time alone. It is precisely at this moment when the boss notices a fly in his inkwell. He plays with/tortures the fly until it dies. After the fly's death, the boss is even more upset.

The central character in "The Fly" is the boss. He seems to be intent on changing things, his desk, his carpet, his office, but the one furnishing which he always keeps is the picture of his son. He keeps the picture, although he "did not draw old Woodifield's attention to the photograph over the table of a grave-looking boy in uniform standing in one of those spectral photographer's parks with photographer's storm-clouds behind him. It was not new. It had been there for over six years" (598). The boss had dearly loved his son. He had created the business for his son to take over upon his death. However, fate held different cards. The boy was killed in the war, thus destroying any dreams the father had for his son. It had taken the father a long time to adjust to the untimely death of his son. The boss then plays a God-like role with a fly. Since he was "the boss" (Mansfield never gives the character a name), he manipulated the fly with ink. He pushed the fly to its physical limits, and then finally killed it. He did not understand any sense of limitation.

The central conflict in "The Fly" lies within the psyche of the boss. He gloats when old Mr. Woodifield is in his office because he wants Mr. Woodifield to know that the boss in in control. It gives him "a feeling of deep, solid satisfaction" (601). However, even though the boss projects this persona, he cannot control everything. He had controlled his son. He had created the business for his son. But his son had been taken away from him.

Mansfield uses a new technique in this story. She writes part of it in the first person. When she writes "we cling to our last pleasures as a tree clings to its last leaves" (597), she is foreshadowing what is about to take place. To be in control is what pleasure the boss has. The boss tries to measure the resiliency of the fly by pushing it to its absolute physical limits. He thinks, "That was the way to tackle things; that was the right spirit" (601). When he finally sees the fly die, by the action of his own hand, he is reminded of his own mortality, and he becomes frightened. He orders new blotting paper and tells Macey, his secretary, to "look sharp about it." He is reminded of his own mortality by the discussion of the son; he sees that he is growing older and more forgetful like Mr. Woodifield; and he realizes that even though he is the boss, he cannot control everything. All of these reminders which occur in the boss' psyche cause him to become frightened—frightened of old age, senility and death.

"*A Married Man's Story*"

"A Married Man's Story" offers an unfinished psychological sketch, an attempt at probing the identity of a man in a dysfunctional marriage. Mansfield presents the man's condition as if it is a typical psychological case, a common malady among males. As if writing in a diary or, at times, speaking from a psychiatrist's couch, the man recounts his inability to feel for his wife or child; he confesses to events which, though terrifying to him when they happened, seem not unlike the traumas that shape most people. Using a brooding, gothic tone to convey the dark, repressed side of human conscience, Mansfield apparently wishes to assert that such common traumas have adverse effects on many men. The man's description of his mother, for whose bed-ridden life he blames himself, becomes the most important image in the story; Mansfield develops a parallel between his mother and his wife, who lies "in her cold bed, staring into the dark" (614). Then, the man reveals his fear that his father poisoned his mother; his fear, implies Mansfield, has emasculated him, made him wary of every man's ability to "poison" a marriage. Yet, ironically, he has slain his own marriage by clinging to his anxiety.

Like a Gothic Monster, the narrator wallows in the darkest parts of his conscience. He enjoys the night, he says; he enjoys "the tide of darkness rising" (620). The darkness gives him a pleasant sense of "drifting," a feeling of numbness and oblivion, like a security blanket that helps the child forget his fears. He also believes that his affinity for darkness is evident to everyone, and that it was particularly evident to his childhood acquaintances: "No wonder I was hated at school. Even the masters shrank from me. I somehow knew that my soft hesitating voice disgusted them" (618), as did his "shocked, staring eyes." Yet he has assessed his state enough to be convinced that his mother's ambiguous death has sucked him into his depression. After she lay on his bed at midnight and whispered that his father had poisoned her, the narrator turned to the night for security, as if he were its child. He began to lie in it, as his mother had lain in her bed for years after his birth. And, as if inheriting a role from his father, he now suffocates his marriage with his disturbance.

The narrator suffers especially under the uncertainty of whether his mother died of poisoning. Was he dreaming what his mother told him? If her premortal visit were real, was the poisoning literal, or was she making a figurative statement, a declaration that she was suffering under oppression? Certainly Mansfield is drawing a parallel between the narrator and his father. The narrator realizes that his marriage is as unhappy for his wife as for him. He remarks that his wife cannot be a proper mother and implies that her failure in the roles of woman perhaps is due to the devouring psychological darkness surrounding her. He describes her eyes as "like the eyes of a cow that is being driven along a road." " 'Why am I being driven—what harm have I done?' " (621). Although he denies responsibility for her sadness, he ironically implies that he is oppressing her, forcing his depression upon her. Indeed, he is lying as he absolves himself. Emotionally, his wife is already dead, like his mother. Mansfield then implies a more complex parallel: she leaves the reader to wonder if the narrator's child will experience a trauma similar to his own. Will this psychological ghoul haunt generations to come?

"The Dove's Nest"

Milly and her mother and Marie the maid live in the French Riviera. They consume coffee, air, and chat idly, and are happy to the extent that they are not ostensibly morose, which is surprising since their lives are extraordinarily bereft of meaning. Mr. Prodger, a visitor from America stops in unexpectedly one day asking to see the man of the house. But because Katherine Mansfield wrote this story (though she never finished it), that man is dead, has been dead for two years. But the ladies invite the Prodger back to lunch and this composes the plot of the story—the time building toward the luncheon and the luncheon itself. The characters do not interact in any important ways, nor do they in their several voltages of isolation enact any memorable dramas, achieve any new frontiers of introspection, or exhibit any familiar human emotion or motivation.

Yet each is disconcertingly engaging. Miss Anderson, the vaguely moral figure and Mother's companion since her husband's death, plods through the house like an ubiquitous spook, caresses people's faces with fingers "cold, pale, like church candles" (623). Marie wags her "sausage finger" before her nose and corrects everyone else's French. And for her, handing potatoes to Miss Anderson at dinner is like "handing potatoes to a corpse" (629). Milly fears the day when Miss Anderson will ask her about God, but until then, Milly has her own incorruptible world of phantasms and her innocent, girlish fantasies. She says, "The ice-cream I adore ice-cream" (636). "Do you?" said Mr. Prodger, and he put down his fork; he seemed moved. "So you're fond of ice-cream, are you Miss Fawcett?" (636). Milly transferred her dazzling gaze to him. It said she was.

If "The Dove's Nest" has to be about something (and one certainly gets the sense that it does not) then it must be about the comedy and tragedy of unused nervous energy, of static tension. And there is a great deal of sexual tension here, between Milly and Mr. Prodger, Mother and Mr. Prodger, Marie and Mr. Prodger, and even Miss Anderson and Milly. But Mansfield avoids allowing her narrative to degenerate into a study of gender roles. Instead, she examines power as a dimension of companionship, only that companionship is displaced by a narrative that merely implies those necessary human bonds that *comprise* family, never demonstrates them. KM strains to write this story. She wants to write a series of first-person narrations, wants to write monologues, but realizes that her characters have only inarticulate notions of themselves and could scarcely manage muted impressions of each other. That Mr. Prodger loves hot-plates or that Marie would love to visit America or that Milly adores ice-cream and the sun and orchids mean absolutely nothing on their own. That these people live in terror of not being thus enamored or engaged means everything.

The dove's nest is a place of comfort and security. Everyone in this story is searching for it. Mansfield makes very sure that each believes he/she has found it, and makes us equally sure she/he has not.

"Six Years After"
The narrator of "Six Years After" is an older woman traveling with her husband whom she calls "Daddy." She begins with a mental description of how pleasant being aboard ship would be during the foul weather if she was tucked away in her cabin with "a rug, a hot water bottle and a piping hot cup tea" (638), but we

learn that she is not going to her cabin. She is huddled under a rug in a deck chair beside her husband, freezing because he believes it is easier for her to "make these sacrifices than it (is) for him" (639). As she sits, she contemplates the sea, and she begins to think of her son whom the title suggests has been dead six years. She daydreams of his life as if he were still alive—a wedding, a grandchild—and works herself into a state of despair. "I can't bear it!" she exclaims and tosses off her blanket (642). The story ends at this point.

Like most of Mansfield's male characters, Daddy is an insensitive man who does not consider the needs of his wife and evokes no sympathy from the reader. Although he is called "Daddy," he behaves more like a child than a father. He subordinates his wife's needs to his own, and knowing that what he is doing is wrong, demands her approval to ease his conscience. He is also "childishly" proud of his expensive cap, and he is childishly defensive. Although Mansfield devotes most of the story to the interactions between the narrator and her husband, the character who has the most impact on the narrator's emotions is her deceased son. The narrator and her husband have been married 28 years, yet she cannot communicate with him, and the prevailing images are of loneliness—silence, gulls, and the barren sea. Looking out over the rainy sea, the narrator grapples with her conflict between life and death, love and absence of love. She is sitting beside her living husband who fails to give her love, and thinking of her deceased son who did love her. For a long time she has been asking herself, "Can one do nothing for the dead?" and the answer has been "Nothing!" In this story, however, she seems to find a solution. She thinks, "There is nothing to be gained by waiting," and moments later throws off her blanket in spite of the bitter cold (642). Although the story ends here, it seems that she is about to do something irreparable: expose herself to cold and illness or throw herself into the sea.

The story is about loss and death; however, in a broader sense, it is an indictment of the position of women in early twentieth-century society and those who accept it. Both Daddy and the narrator are guilty of accepting and thereby reinforcing the social norm. Daddy knows he is not treating his wife fairly, but justifies his behavior by thinking it is a law of marriage, and the narrator encourages his behavior through her silence. Although she is obviously very cold, she merely says, "I shall be glad of my rug" (638). Given their mutual acceptance of the unequal relationship, the narrator's only escape is death.

"All Serene"

Mansfield in "All Serene" peers into the deceptively perfect world of a young "ideal" couple—the Rutherfords. Theirs is a fastidiously stylized world—a world of charming breakfasts filled with loving exchanges of contentment, a world of artful displays— of smiles, of caresses. But, KM, with harsh, even frightening clarity, shows their world as an illusion—a play, if you will, in which they are both merely acting out roles in a sad drama of mutual self-deception otherwise known as marriage. Their serene world, their blissful marriage is shown to be merely a futile human attempt to give meaning to that which is perhaps meaningless. Thus, Mansfield is calling into question the very existence of what we define as "love" and "marriage."

Mona Rutherford has made a lifetime of convincing herself of the perfection of the love she and her husband, Hugh, share. She has made it her duty to create this illusion—"She thought it part of her duty to him—to their love, even, to wear charming little caps, funny little coats...and to see that the table was as perfect as he and she—fastidious pair!" (653-54). With dramatic flair they exchange what seems to be a practiced, memorized dialogue of love. They use the same perfected, mannered performances every day, and indeed they are quite convincing—"There was the look on his face she loved—a kind of sweet jesting. He was pretending.... He was pretending to be feeling" (654). In order to sustain this extended drama they each agree not to read the other's mail because she "always get(s) mysterious epistles from girls (she was) at college with or faded aunts" (654) and he receives letters of invitation that look "awfully unbusinesslike" with "funny writing—much more like a woman's than a man's" (656). But of course, they never suspect each other. Their relationship is far too filled with deep admiration and awe over their happiness for suspicion. They both wear masks. Mona, however, seems to be at least somewhat aware of this, but would never admit it to anyone, including herself. She, like a blind director of a play, plans out her every move, watching but not ever really seeing her true "self." In a moment of reflection on her life, she realizes she has lost her identity and has become a mere persona. "She seemed to be showing their house and him to her other self, the self she had been before she had met him. Deeply admiring, almost awed by so much happiness, that other self looked on..." (657). Mona has willingly given in to the role she requires of herself.

The story, in raw, unfinished, and displeasurable terms, explores the disparity between love and deception. KM forcefully suggests that deception is the mode society has chosen to live by, that "love" and "marriage" are merely smaller elements in the larger drama of life—a drama which bases itself on posing and play-acting, a drama which uses beauty, smiles, caresses, pleasantries to blind people to the reality of a base world governed by little more than one's own appetites. We are charmed by love in order to forget our true selves, to forget the stage we are acting upon. In a moment of revelation Mona looks at her house—her dramatic world, and realizes—"It was like a stage setting with the curtain still down. She had no right to be there" (658). But her role is fixed and she will not give it up. She has no identity and cannot gain one. For Mona, like most individuals, deception is much easier. We would rather be blind, identityless creatures inhabiting our roles without ever looking for the director or the writer—without understanding ourselves or the play we act in.

"Susannah"

Mansfield's "Susannah" is an unfinished short story, offered for the reader in two versions. From what is written, "Susannah" seems to be concerned with one young girl's experience of going to the fair. Knowing KM, this experience will probably not turn out well for the child, but we cannot know for sure. The two versions are roughly equivalent in length and share many common characteristics, including the main character and secondary characters. The plot concepts are also very similar. In each version of the story the "kind generous Father" (670) has made it possible for his three daughters to attend the Exhibition or Fair, and the girls are preparing to go.

The main character is the youngest of the three daughters, Susannah. This is no real surprise, since Mansfield is the youngest of three daughters. Also, Susannah's father shares many characteristics of Mansfield's father, including the high reverence with which the family is supposed to regard his hardworking, "generous" nature. In both versions of the story, Susannah is shown to be a "naughty, ungrateful child" who does not appreciate all the wonderful sacrifices her father makes for her. The first version concerns itself with Susannah's ungratefulness much less, only approaching the issue directly when Susannah quite matter-of-factly states that her father does not work everyday, he takes off on Saturday afternoons and Sundays. Her mother's shocked indignation is our sign that Susannah is being "naughty." In the second version, however, this seems much more to be the story. The second version ends with Susannah bowing down in shame after her parents have misinterpreted her fear of the fair as ungrateful behavior. Susannah's fear is also a major issue in the second version of "Susannah." It seems to be a major cause in Susannah's clash with her parents. The first version, however, only gives the reader a hint of Susannah's fear, making it seem all the more ominous. "But Susannah looked as though falling over had no terror for her. On the contrary" (671). Mansfield makes a paragraph of these two sentences, adding to the ominous nature. It seems as if she planned to expand on this fear. In any case, both versions portray Susannah as an "ungrateful" child who has the natural reaction of being afraid of the fair.

The conflict in each version, then, would seem to be concerned with the same concepts, Susannah's fear, and her parents' consequent misinterpretation. The angle from which Mansfield is approaching the conflict, however, seems to be different for each version. The first version seems as if it would be the most ominous and threatening one. Everything, on the surface, seems so happy; the children are so excited. Except Susannah is a little afraid. Sounds scary. Mansfield is setting up the reader too well for this story to turn out happily. In the second version, we already get a hint of the conflict before KM quits writing. This version is very emotional and ends with a quite pitiful picture of a young girl almost bowing down before her father to "beg for his forgiveness" (672). Maybe this version was just too difficult for Mansfield to write. Since neither of the plot conflicts is resolved, we can only guess how either of these versions would have turned out. However, knowing what we do about Mansfield and her life, it is likely that this would have been one very unhappy ending.

"Weak Heart"

Katherine Mansfield's "Weak Heart" is also an unfinished story. Begun in November of 1921, Mansfield wrote in her journal: "To-day I begin to write, seriously, 'The Weak Heart'—a story which fascinates me *deeply*. What I feel it needs so peculiarly is a subtle variation of tense from the present to the past and back again—and softness, lightness, and the feeling that all is in bud, with a ply of humour over the character of Roddie" (Murry 388-89). But ill-health and general dissatisfaction with her work caused Mansfield to abandon the story until she felt more clear about her purpose. Time ran out, however, and a little more than a year later she was dead. What remains of the story is the complete beginning, notes on what might have happened in the middle, and the ending, written according to J. Middleton Murry, "at top speed" (389). Whether or not the finished story would have contained a "subtle variation of tense" is difficult to say, but the work does have a feeling of spring to it, as it begins with a description of the violets in the Bengel's garden and the general flowering of the yards all along Tarana Street. The sound of Edie Bengel's piano adds to the blossoming of the street and its plaintive air causes passers-by to stop and gaze thoughtfully at the house and garden.

The sounds of the piano reflect Edie's emotional state—she is full of desperate longing to live life to the fullest, to be allowed to join Miss Farmer's girls, whose presence in church often fascinated her. But some tragedy must have been planned to occur in the middle of the story, for it ends with Edie's funeral as it is watched by Roddie. He exits suddenly from the graveside to dash up to the house, thinking wildly that he will find Edie at her accustomed place, but she is not there, as the frozen piano mockingly seems to say.

The main character in "Weak Heart" is Edie Bengel, an adolescent girl who seems isolated from her peers, probably because of her delicate condition. But like most young girls, Edie is eager to begin fully living life, to enjoy her developing mind and body. Her situation is comparable to the season at the beginning of the story; like the springtime, Edie is bursting with new life and vigor. She is on the verge of young womanhood, about to ripen into full summer. But as the flowers of spring are threatened by a sudden frost, so is Edie threatened by her weak heart. She pours out her frustrations and longings on the piano, playing by memory, until she is flushed with exertion and her heart beats rapidly. Her piano playing is also Edie's way of praying, and what she wants most in the world is to be allowed to attend Miss Farmer's school for girls, to join with the other girls in that beehive of activity she has passed so often, and to learn the names of the pupils she has seen in church. Yet for some reason the unfinished story does not make clear, unless it is her death which cuts off her chances, Edie never goes to Miss Farmer's school. She might have taken comfort in her friend Roddie, who is mentioned in some notes which are all that is left of the middle of the story. Mansfield cryptically writes, "Edie never knew that Roddie 'loved' it, Roddie never knew that it meant anything to Edie" (682). They apparently share some special bond.

The main conflict as it is laid out in the beginning of the story is between Edie's desire to live and her knowledge that her weak heart will one day kill her. It is as though her piano is her substitute voice, for it can pour out all the frustration and longing Edie feels without its heart suffering. The piano is eloquent and passionate; it can seize life and attention the way Edie can't. It is the piano that makes the passers-by on the street stop to listen, and the piano which sounds throughout the silent house, "frightening, so bold, so defiant, so reckless it rolls under Edie's fingers" (681). The piano demands the answers to the questions of existence. "Ah, if life must pass so quickly, why is the breath of these flowers so sweet? What is the meaning of this feeling of longing, of sweet trouble—of flying joy?" (680). Edie must see the lovers who parade into the shadow of the velvet tree on Tarana Street, and wonder if she will ever get the chance to do the same. After her death, her conflict is mirrored in Roddie's mad dash from the cemetery to find her. This young boy, so full of life, cannot believe that Edie, who was the same, could be dead. But on behalf of all that is delightful, the piano replies. "There is nobody here of that name, young man!" (683).

Chapter Seven

Stories from the Posthumous Collection

Something Childish and Other Stories (1924)

John Middleton Murry's excuse for printing all of KM's final work does not apply to *Something Childish and Other Stories* or to his reprinting of *In a German Pension*, Mansfield's first collection. *Something Childish* is an apt title for the collection, for it contains, along with *German Pension*, some of KM's juvenalia. Six of the 25 stories in the book were written before *German Pension*, but what makes them and other stories in this volume of juvenalia is their "youthful bitterness and crude cynicism" (Murry 695). Some of these stories, such as "The Woman at the Store," are exercises in a genre—the murder mystery—that KM later abandoned. Murry writes in his introduction: "I have no doubt that Katherine Mansfield, were she still alive, would not have suffered some of these stories to appear" (523).

Time and maturity had taught KM that the way to reach a more sophisticated audience was to write on more universal themes, and to temper her outlook on life and humanity with pity and understanding. KM did not like to be reminded of her earlier faults, and she thought that the publication of these earlier works would denigrate her later work with which she was more satisfied. But Murry's opinion, which he had expressed to KM in 1920 when the success of *Bliss* made publishers want to reprint *In a German Pension*, was that a writer could not "annihilate" any work he or she did not like by refusing to have it reprinted (696). Mansfield would placate Murry by promising to write a new introduction to *In a German Pension* if the time ever came to reprint it, with a warning to the public that she was "not like that anymore" (Murry 523). But death cut off her wishes, and Murry did what he thought best.

In her will, KM left all her papers to Murry with the instructions: "I should like him to publish as little as possible and tear up and burn as much as possible" (Alpers 341). Murry was

114

therefore left with a difficult decision—what exactly was as little or as much as possible, according to KM? Also, what did he owe to KM as her husband and lover, and how much to the scholarly world as her editor? Murry really could not win, whatever he chose to do. If he published all that was left of her work, even the fragments, there are those who could claim that he denied her wishes and destroyed her privacy, or like D.H. Lawrence, could assert that Murry was asking the public to buy KM's "waste-paper basket" (Tomalin 239). If he honored her wishes and destroyed her work, scholars would be outraged, and this might hurt Mansfield's reputation. My own opinion is that I am glad that Murry printed these works, for many of them are quite worth reading and studying, and it is also informative to chart KM's progress as a writer. What Mansfield wanted was for these works to be read in their proper context, and anyone who has read a representative of her work knows that, as Cherry Hankin has said, KM matured as a writer from *In a German Pension* to *The Garden Party*, but one can still appreciate the distinctive style that Mansfield gave to all her works.

"The Tiredness of Rosabel"

In "The Tiredness of Rosabel," Rosabel is a young London milliner, tired from a hard workday and heading home on the bus, after forsaking dinner in order to buy violets. A girl nearby is reading a romance novel, as Rosabel daydreams. Having reached her humble room, she reflects on the day's event, including her experiences with a rich and handsome young couple: the woman leaves the man to pay for her hat, and he suggestively compliments Rosabel as well. She constructs her own fairy-tale romance with him, in which she possesses all the luxury and beauty she could never have in reality. Her fatigue sends her to bed, still optimistic and smiling in the gloom and grime of her existence.

The dichotomy between the rich young woman and Rosabel, that between the "haves" and "have nots," is obvious. The fact that both women are exploited is perhaps less apparent. Although Rosabel's fantasy of wealth seems to sustain her in her poverty, its effect is not positive but self-destructive in its perpetuation of repressive societal norms and stereotypes for women, regardless of social status. Rosabel's fatigue contributes to her willingness to engage in a utopian fantasy. While her feelings of discontent are momentarily pacified, Rosabel subconsciously validates the status quo and her continued exploitation by fantasizing herself among those who are responsible for her present condition. At issue, however, is not just social class but gender as well. Just as violets are objects of beauty to be possessed, so are women represented in both Rosabel's real and fantasized lives.

Mansfield's bitter irony succeeds in portraying the evils of "opiates," that which oppressors use to intoxicate and thereby control others. The exploration of the female consciousness and of women's roles in society is the enlightened view of the experienced.

"How Pearl Button Was Kidnapped"

Mansfield's "How Pearl Button Was Kidnapped" is a story about a little girl named Pearl Button who is kidnapped by two strange women. One day while Pearl is playing in the front yard, swinging on the gate and singing a song, two barefooted women approach Pearl and question the whereabouts of her mother. Pearl tells them that her mother is in the kitchen ironing. When they realize that Pearl is alone, they ask her if she wants to go with them. And being alone, longing for some company, Pearl accepts their invitation and begins her journey with the mysterious strangers. Possibly, this is a dream that Pearl is having, because she is watching the clouds that are playing hide-and-seek, and perhaps Pearl drifts into the clouds and these women are the ones who find her.

Pearl Button, the main character, is a lonely little girl who enjoys playing in a make-believe world and talking to people. She has a very beautiful, appealing smile. This is one reason why people enjoy talking to her; they are fascinated by her smile. Pearl is also a very inquisitive child who finds great interest in asking and answering questions. She is very well trained, courteous, and above all a quite intelligent child. Pearl spends most of her time playing by herself. This is another indicator that Pearl's kidnapping could be a dream that Pearl drifts into from pure loneliness. Whatever the circumstance, Pearl very willingly goes along with the two women.

The conflict arises in the story when Pearl decides to go along with the two women so she can find out what they have in their House of Boxes. As they walk, Pearl becomes very tired, so one of the women picks up Pearl and carries her the remainder of the journey. When they reach the ladies' house, Pearl is placed in a room filled with men; they find her to be the cutest little girl in the world. They are very friendly towards Pearl, and she is having the time of her life. Pearl suddenly becomes very hungry and one of the men takes a peach out of his pocket and rolls it to Pearl. Being the courteous little girl that she is, Pearl asks for permission to eat the peach. The men find Pearl very amusing, and in the midst of all the laughter, Pearl gets very excited and squirts juice from the peach all over herself.

She is frightened that she has done something wrong, but the women assure her that everything is okay. Later they continue their journey, but this time their destination is by the sea. There she sees little houses with wooden fences surrounding them, red and blue clothes hanging on the fences, yellow dogs, and above all fat people who are running around carrying naked babies. Pearl also sees a little girl who is setting the dinner table, and Pearl questions the whereabouts of the little girl's House of Boxes. Pearl is later taken closer to the sea where she becomes very frightened by the waves. After one of the ladies calms her down, Pearl joins in with the people who are collecting shells. In the process, Pearl suddenly falls and becomes very upset. Suddenly she is picked up by some little blue men who carry her back to the House of Boxes. This is possibly the end of Pearl's dream. At any rate, it is the end of this youthful KM fantasy as short story.

"A Truthful Adventure"

The titles of Katherine Mansfield's short stories usually reflect an important theme or idea from the story, encapsulating in a few words the essence of the story. "A Truthful Adventure" is no exception, for the story concerns a woman traveler named Katherine who happens to be from New Zealand. This story was written in conjunction with "The Journey to Bruges," according to Antony Alpers, when Mansfield visited that city in 1911 (Alpers 142). Mansfield, with her sardonic eye always open to ironic possibilities, records her experiences in Bruges, which don't always meet her expectations. The story opens with a description of Bruges taken from a guidebook, promising "silver canals" and "fantastic dreams." What Katherine finds is no room at the hotel, sleepy waiters, revolting pink bedrooms, noisy neighbors, garrulous boatmen, and fat tourists who insist on honing in on her boat ride.

What she had hoped to find was peace and quiet, floating alone down the silver canals, or lying in the long grass of the Beguinage meadow, "and growing full enough of grace to last me the whole winter" (18). Her reverie, though interrupted by the fat woman tourist's fall into the canal, is finally shattered when an old school friend from New Zealand whom Katherine barely remembers spots her lying on the grass in the meadow and immediately starts pestering her to join her and her husband on their tours around the city, and for Katherine to give her opinion on the Suffrage, which she and her husband are keen on. This is enough to make Katherine reply that she has been called away suddenly by an emergency.

The main character in "A Truthful Adventure" is Katherine, who seems to be an independent-minded traveler. She has not come to Bruges to be pushed and prodded from one historical site to the next like a regular tourist, but prefers to go her own way at her own pace. Her flexibility is indicated by her willingness to accept accommodation at Madame's private residence when the hotel is full. Yet for all her independence, Katherine has a romantic side to her which is inspired by the description of Bruges in the guidebook: "It sounded extremely comforting, and my tired heart, tucked away under a thousand and one grey city wrappings, woke and exulted within me..." (18). She feels as though she can renew her soul in Bruges and she tries not to let the few disappointments which occur set her back. So what if the room is ugly and the neighbors complain of their feet? There are still the canals to explore.

Then, when the canal trip becomes a disaster, Katherine still believes she can find her "grace" lying in the Beguinage meadow, despite the crowds of artists and vulgar English girls throwing candy and cigarettes. But Katherine cannot remain an optimist in the face of cold, hard reality, which takes the shape of an old school friend who insists on renewing old times which Katherine would rather forget. She quickly decides that Bruges is a loss, and the best thing to do would be to leave immediately.

The major conflict in "A Truthful Adventure" centers on Katherine's wish to find in the old city of Bruges a place untouched by the chaos of the modern world, where she can rest and refresh her spirit. The guidebook seems to promise this in its description of Bruges: "Life is long since asleep in Bruges; fantastic dreams alone breathe over tower and medieval house front" (18). Katherine is searching for a kind of religious regeneration, for the kind of faith found in the medieval era, as she dreams of lying in the Beguinage meadow at evensong, listening to the nuns at prayer, and feeling herself growing in grace. But even as Katherine is soaring aloft on the wings of her dreams, the modern world intrudes and brings her down with a thump. The Bruges of medieval times is gone for good, replaced by a tourist industry which reduces the timeless beauty of the city to a money-making concern. The hotel owner will only find a room for Katherine because she proposes to stay for an extended period of time. She is told that she must have a guide for exploring the canals, who ruins the experience by chattering incessantly, not to mention the low comedy of the fat tourists. The peace of the Beguinage meadow has been replaced by the shrieks of the English tourists and the legs of countless easels. With the appearance of an over-zealous schoolmate, Katherine realizes her dream was just that, a dream, and she plans to depart Bruges, probably a little sadder, but wiser.

"The Woman at the Store"

In "The Woman at the Store," three travelers meet an odd woman while traveling cross-country. The travelers—Jo, Jim, and an unnamed female narrator—stop at a rural store after a hard day of traveling. The woman, who lives at the store with her little girl, says that her husband is away shearing sheep. The woman reluctantly allows the travelers to stay the night. The travelers spend the night in the store while Jo sleeps with the women. Jim and the narrator find out from the little girl that the woman killed her husband. When Jim and the narrator leave, Jo stays behind and says he will catch up later. As Jim and the narrator ride around the bend, the store disappears from view.

Loneliness is an important element in this story. The woman at the store kills her husband after he left her alone for long periods of time. Loneliness pushed her over the edge. Jo also has to deal with loneliness. Jo attempts to alleviate his loneliness by staying with the woman. Even the little girl is lonely. She has no friends and so she has to draw pictures both to entertain and express herself. The theme of death runs alongside the idea of loneliness. Mansfield uses loneliness and death to create a gloomy atmosphere, and to show how desolate the lives of Jo and the woman at the store have become.

Mansfield uses elements of the gothic to accentuate the theme of death. The murder of the husband and the dark stormy night provide the gothic elements. "The Woman at the Store" is essentially a parody of gothic stories. Although they possess dark, mysterious elements, gothic stories tended to end with a romantic, optimistic event. Instead of romance and optimism, Mansfield ends her story with despair and desperation. This despair and desperation, combined with the theme of death, are devices KM uses to present a grim story of one woman's anguish and loneliness.

"Ole Underwood"

This is a very sad story, delineating deep suffering through the character portrayal of Ole Underwood. His life, filled with grief and misfortune, finally leads to the unbearable affliction of mental illness. The setting is Wellington, a site known for its gusty winds and port facilities. The narrator uses the "windy air" as a backdrop to paint a picture of Ole as he walks stiffly towards town, clothed in a black cape and hat, carrying a black umbrella in one hand and his red and white knotted handkerchief in the other. Marked by inner fear, Ole often experiences a rapid heartbeat and pulse rate. The narrator describes the sound as "a thud…like someone beating on an iron in a prison…a secret place—bang—trying to get free" (135). This "beat" in his chest represents a physiological sign indicative of Ole's anxiety. As he approaches the town, he passes "ugly little houses," and he is sneered at by two residents. When he reaches the pub in the heart of town, he is taunted by the bar maid, and his life's story is free-spoken by a man in the pub; Ole hears this conversation, and he reacts by crushing the "red pinks."

Of course, he is immediately kicked out of the pub. He continues to walk around the town.

Looking intently and fixedly through a window at the Chinamen playing cards, Ole decides to enter the shop. He opens the door as carefully as he can; however, the strong, gusty wind from the outside scatters the Chinamen's cards. With a loud, piercing "Ya-Ya!," the Chinamen frighten Ole away. Just as Ole flees the pub after being kicked onto the street, he scurries away from the little shop into a timber yard. As he lay there gasping, a gray cat befriends him while "waving her tail." He warmly refers to the cat as "Kit," for this is the name his wife gave the cat he brought to her off his ship. As he reflects on his wife and his days as a sailor, his "heart beat madly." Protecting the cat inside his coat, Ole moves with an awkward, slouching posture to the woodyards. He smells a horrible odor coming from the sewage into the sea. This awful smell agitates and confuses his sensory perception. Looking at the wharves and the ships with flying flags, Ole is extremely excited as "the old, old lust" swept over him. In a low, angry voice the giddy Underwood mutters "I will! I will! I will!" (137). At this moment, he takes the cat out by her tail and swings her into the sewer.

For a moment, Ole imagines he is young again. As he walks along the wharves, he notices a "little ship." Before going aboard, he looks back at the dismal town, the dark clouds, the red prison. The narrator describes a mad man, a mentally unbalanced man, who "grinned and rolled in his walk..." (138) as he finally goes on board the vessel. Ole exhibits irrationality and mental unsoundness for he believes that the ship belongs to him; in fact, he imagines himself to be the man sleeping in the bunk—"A great big man in a seaman's coat..." (138). The smiling woman on the picture is his wife. She is smiling, in his eyes no doubt, at him.

One cannot help but pity the mentally deranged character Mansfield creates in this short story. The "gusty wind" as well as all the colors provide insight for character description. To begin, the color of Ole's attire, which is black, permeates the story. The black attire and the black "webby clouds" create a gloomy mood. One knows immediately that something disastrous is taking place. The grey sky, the grey cat, and the grey water symbolize the dull and dismal view that others take toward him. As he strutted into

town with his chest extended it is ironic, for it is definitely
incongruent with the way he is treated by the townspeople. For
instance, the woman who shook her "red soapy fist" as he passed
her house, and the red-haired waitress in the pub who shoved him
a mug clearly indicate that no matter how he tries to carry himself,
he will always be considered a mentally ill person in their sight.
The color red, alone, indicates their anger and resentment towards
Ole.

Both the above-mentioned characters use a form of force
while casting Ole aside to live in complete isolation. Despite his
mental capability, he is sensitive enough to show anger and
resentment, too. Not only is he upset with the pub waitress, he is
equally upset with the man who engages in dialogue with another
about his wife's betrayal, his subsequent act of murder, and his 20-
year prison term. The "red pinks" that he crushes remind him of
the "red" prison. Apparently, the "red" prison is a cause for
embarrassment, if we can believe the dialogue in the pub. Also,
the "thud...like someone beating on an iron in a prison...trying to
be free" (135) indicates Ole's deepest, darkest secret, which will
haunt him for the rest of his life. The narrator reminds us that Ole
is saddened by the sight of the prison on the hill; surely, this is
where loneliness began for him. Wherever he travels in the town,
he always feels a bit awkward, and prefers to remain unnoticed.

Ole enters the pub quietly, hoping to go unnoticed. His
attempt is not successful. In spite of his lowly entrance, head and
shoulders drooping, customers point and nudge one another. While
shuffling away from the pub, a woman drops "a pail of slops on
his feet." Regardless of how careful he tries to be, misfortune
lurks; the Chinamen frightened him away after he carefully
opened the shop door. Ole's derangement occasionally makes him
act childlike. For instance, he "shoos" the chickens and laughs
about it as he walks to town; he presses his face against the glass
shop front and "sniggers" as only a child would do. Ole's persona
is sad and disturbing, for everywhere he goes during the course of
a single day, he demonstrates anger, discontentment and
resentment.

Ole Underwood's struggle is with loneliness and isolation. He
has no acceptance by people in the town because of the violent act
he is said to have committed against his wife. He also struggles

with isolation, for the townspeople are convinced that he "cracked" as a result of years of imprisonment; therefore, they will neither accept him nor will they forgive him. Although some say he is harmless, such as the man in the pub, no one seems willing to accept him as a friend or an associate. His mental derangement culminates as he makes his way back to the wharves, the sea, and finally the boat on which he imagines the sleeping seaman to be himself with his wife's smiling picture hanging on the wall of the stateroom. It is possible that Mansfield could have meant the struggle or conflict to be interpreted differently. If so, then perhaps the sleeping seaman is the man who caused his wife's betrayal, and he still keeps her picture on the wall over his bunk. The latter interpretation seems unlikely. Ole's damaged mentality and isolation seem to be at issue in this story.

"Something Childish But Very Natural"

"Something Childish But Very Natural" may strike a reader as one of Mansfield's weakest stories. Please also see my very different interpretation of this story in Chapter Two. Yes, sometimes even a fairly simple story can have radically different interpretations. Biographer Claire Tomalin in *Katherine Mansfield: A Secret Life* agrees, calling the story "vapid," and writes that at the time, 1914, Mansfield was "worried about her writing becoming 'pretty-pretty,' with some reason..." (Tomalin 125). The one characteristic that is made crystal clear about the two flat characters—a trait that is reiterated time and time again— is their childishness. The reader could stomach Edna's and Henry's childishness if there appeared in the story sustained irony or a resolution suggesting self-discovery as is often found in other Mansfield stories which deal with child-like characters. "Bliss" comes to mind with its immature protagonist experiencing a sexual awakening as well as discovering her husband's infidelity. No such discovery occurs in "Something Childish But Very Natural," although the reader familiar with Mansfield's later stories keeps expecting an ironic twist. And the writer does seem to suggest in places that something will happen, but nothing ever does.

One finishes the story and wonders what the point of it all is. Before going further, though, let's summarize the story. By accident Henry encounters Edna on a commuter train leaving London one evening. Struck by her "marigold-colored hair," he arranges to meet her again. Three days later they share a train compartment and, chatting, discover they are both 17 and think alike. Henry and Edna fall in love. The young lovers go to concerts, explore the city, and claim a village as their own. The couple is delightfully happy except that Edna does not want Henry to touch her because she believes that if he does, their relationship will change. One day, after a long walk, they chance upon a cottage for rent, and as they wander through the house, imagining it as theirs, Edna throws her arms around Henry's neck. Everything, as Henry says, seems " 'perfect, perfect, perfect' " (181). But in the final scene while Henry waits for Edna at the cottage, he receives a telegram brought by a little girl. And here the story ends. The telegram might or might not have been from Edna; it might or might not have informed him that she wouldn't be coming. On these points Mansfield remains mum.

Time and again KM underscores the characters' childishness. Henry and Edna are both 17, but in appearance, speech, and action they seem to be seven years old. Henry's straw hat, for example, pinches him so he wonders if his head has grown larger since the previous summer; the detail suggests that Henry is still a growing boy, not yet at his full height. Edna wears her yellow hair as a young girl would. Alluded to is the custom of women putting up their hair when they begin working or marry, though Henry remarks that Edna will behave differently. Imagining their future life, he says, " 'though we're married you refuse to put your hair up and only tuck it inside your coat for the church service' " (172). In Henry's spoken wish for Edna to remain a child, the reader can also detect an unwillingness on his part to accept mature responsibilities. Edna's speech likewise illustrates her desire to remain a child. In fact, the reason for her not wanting to touch Henry is tied directly to this vain hope of forever being a girl. " 'Somehow I feel if once we did that...held each other's hands and kissed it would all be changed'," she explains. " 'We wouldn't be children anymore' " (174). Her actions also reveal Edna to be as fickle as any child; she reverses her "no touching" rule and throws her arms around Henry's neck but then, later, changes her mind yet again and doesn't appear for their weekend at the cottage. Henry's actions are no less childish than hers. As he waits for Edna at the cottage he imagines the night to come. His imaginings (his intended actions), however, don't revolve around sexual fantasies, as the reader would expect from a young man of 17, but instead lead to Henry's and Edna's retiring to separate beds in separate rooms. Although Mansfield provides many more, these illustrations suffice in establishing the couple's childishness, but the question then becomes for what purpose are these one-sided, childish characters presented?

An obvious answer is that Mansfield creates the two as the butt of her satire, a technique she employs in other stories, most notably her later one, "Taking the Veil." And clues from "Something Childish But Very Natural" support this interpretation—but only so far. For example, the title, borrowed from a poem that Henry reads at a bookstall, can be read as ironic. The verses themselves are fatuous, built around a central image of "a little feathery bird" flying to its lover, and the fact that Henry finds the poem moving alerts the reader to the inherent irony. Henry, who is not a critical reader, fails to detect the maudlin aspect of the poem and therefore will fail to see that same element in his relationship with Edna. That the pair's relationship is described as "natural" is further evidence of irony. If we understand the bond between lovers as a progression toward greater intimacy, a narrowing of distance, then Henry's and Edna's relationship is not "natural," for it has been arrested at an early stage when the distance between the two is still great. Therefore, the tone of intimacy that the couple affects rings false.

Yet despite the evident discrepancy in how the characters view themselves and how the reader sees them, Mansfield, for her part, seems to be sitting on the fence. True, she sets up irony in the story, but the ironic elements prove sparse and insufficient for the reader trying to determine the writer's feeling towards her characters. It is not clear, as it is in "Taking the Veil," that Mansfield intends to satirize those who attempt to remain children. Does this mean that to a degree she sympathizes with Henry and Edna and is presenting their child-like relationship as a model? If that were her intention, then the use of irony seems inappropriate and misleading to the reader. The ending of the story also raises questions about a sympathetic interpretation of the young lovers.

Does Edna fail to appear at the cottage for the weekend because she, having thrown her arms around Henry's neck and opened the way to greater intimacies, now feels awkward and wishes to revert to their previous, childish relationship? Is Edna's reversion represented by the "little girl in a pinafore" who brings Henry the telegram? And what about Henry who contents himself with innocent and sexless fantasies of the night to come? Is one expected to sympathize with Henry's denial of the telegram's contents? Alerted to the ironic possibilities early in the story, the reader does not know how to answer these questions and is unsure how to interpret "Something Childish But Very Natural." Thus, this problematic story seems one of Mansfield's weakest; it's a case, perhaps, of the writer herself being uncertain of the effect she intended to produce.

"An Indiscreet Journey"

In "An Indiscreet Journey," perhaps one of Mansfield's most complex stories, the reader is unwillingly taken on a voyage into a type of human wasteland. The English narrator, a nameless female, travels from Paris to an unknown destination during wartime in France. She is merely a traveler—a wanderer—moving through time and space without place or identity. Reaching her destination—supposedly the residence of her aunt and uncle, Paul and Julie Boiffard—she meets an expectant young soldier, with whom she moves through this wasteland. They perform meaningless activities together. They sit in cafés. They drink whiskey. They chat idly. Nothing has any significance. Numbness is the only feeling even expressed here. "An Indiscreet Journey," I believe, can be seen as a metaphor for Mansfield's own life—the life of a vagabond—the life of displacement—a life that becomes nothing but a series of meaningless journeys through a world of waste. Her life, like the narrator's, has become a blur, an existence deprived of meaning, and of feeling.

The narrator, an English woman in Paris, lives in a state of perpetual movement. She is running from something, perhaps everything. She lives in disguise, wearing borrowed clothes, leading a borrowed life on borrowed time. She wears an old Burberry—"It did not belong to me. I had borrowed it from a friend.... An old Burberry seems to me the sign and the token of the undisputed venerable traveller" (183). She gains passage on a train and whirls through time—seeing everything in a dreamlike trance it seems—"And now there were soldiers everywhere...And now we were passing big wooden sheds like rigged-up dance halls.... What beautiful cemeteries we are passing!" (185). Passing through this world she has no idea of who she is or what her destination might be—"What is the name of the station where I have to change? Perhaps I shall never know" (185). After arriving at this unnamed place, she merely wanders along with an unnamed soldier-acquaintance who is only defined as "terribly pale, with a faint smile on his lips." During her time here she has nothing to do but "sit in an empty café and listen to a clock ticking" (192).

Having lost the ability to feel and the ability to have a sense of self or place, the narrator merely drifts through life. She has no conflict. Her existence is that of a wayfarer. She is not even searching for anything anymore. The only thing she seeks is movement—perpetual motion. She does not dwell on the past, nor does she look toward the future. She simply lives in the moment. Mansfield perhaps feels that this has become the nature of her own existence. With reserve and certainly more authorial distance than KM customarily uses, she may be exploring her life—her perpetual voyage. She is unsentimental and un-self-pitying throughout the story. The pain and the uncertainty that surely must accompany such a life is never once even mentioned. She does not justify nor does she explain the reasons for her actions. KM simply explores the bare, stark, unapologetic life of the vagabond.

"Late At Night"

Mansfield's "Late At Night" is a dramatic short story written in monologue form. Actually, this is quite a tragic piece. Virginia, sitting by the fire, reads a letter from a male companion who is thanking her for a pair of socks she sent to him. Although he is offering his thanks, he tells her that he recently received five pairs of socks, so he found it fitting to give the pair she sent to a friend. Virginia finds his letter to be cold and piercing; however, she constantly allows herself to make excuses for his remarks. She regrets having written to him and having sent the pair of socks.

Sundays have a very special meaning for Virginia; in fact, it was on a Sunday she wrote to her acquaintance. Admitting that she has not been to church lately, she still finds solace on Sunday evenings while she sits around the fire. As she contemplates church hymns, she feels relief from all grief and the daily anxieties that sometimes overwhelm her being. Generalizing about men, Virginia quickly characterizes them as being disgusting, revolting, and above all repulsive. Virginia admits having known this man for only a short time, but this is really unimportant; apparently it is not unusual behavior for her to shower men with letters and gifts. She confides that men seem to like her "at first," and then they are frightened away by her overbearing personality. She wants to feel loved and need by someone, and she is willing to do almost anything to have the company of a man. Virginia's shallowness peaks through as she tells herself that not only is she special, but she is unique, too. She perceives all men to be "helpless," like "sick animals and birds" (301), and she is forever confident that her loving care will strengthen them. Virginia continues to make excuses for herself and for her friend's letter. Above all, she is simply afraid of growing old alone. She cites age as a factor for her changing ways—"I get cross.... I want to cry" (301). Finally, it is interesting to note that Virginia never destroys the letter. This, too, is a part of her self-delusion. Every time Virginia is about to come to a truth about herself, she says instead "Funny, isn't it?" (300). This allows her to rationalize her character flaws.

The character Virginia is full of complexities. At first glimpse, one is made aware of her shallowness, vanity, and her self-delusion. But upon further examination, her pathology becomes more evident and one begins to realize that her desperate longing for love and her loneliness border on clinical depression. Virginia has quick views of reality, but rather than deal with her inadequacies, she excuses all self-criticism by blaming each negative happening on that over which she has no control. She consistently employs escapism yet knows her weaknesses, which are surely possessiveness and helplessness. The consciousness of this character undergoes several transitions, beginning with the initial emotion of disbelief or at best the lack of certainty about the motivations of her male friend. Initially repelled by his lack of sensitivity and presumptuousness, the emotions escalate into self-recriminations and indignation. She then becomes overwhelmed with self-pity, and she possesses a keen awareness of her deteriorating powers and beauty. The entire atmosphere Virginia creates is one of flux, characterized by shifting emotions that blend into a general mood of ambivalence and uncertainty.

Virginia's struggle to belong to someone is consuming. She yearns to come into bloom: to flower, to again be one with Nature, and most of all to be loved. One thank you note from a male friend describing her gift as one of five similar gifts causes the main conflict. Virginia feels that because he writes that her gift has been duplicated by others is the ultimate "snub." This snub is made even worse because he writes that her "hand-made" gift (a false assumption) was passed on to someone else. Virginia is troubled because she is sure that she wrote the letter on the wrong evening—"Sunday evenings are so fatal" (299). She has a further conflict when he assumes she was fool enough to knit the socks for him—rather than his understanding that she considers herself a discerning, unique shopper. That men find her to be "original" and desirable at first, only later to be repelled by her causes great concern. She is never allowed to display her strong, generous, and boundless love. With age, she finds her once lovely skin, hair and posture declining, and frets over a final fatal worry—"will things never change or if I shall go on like this until I am old..." (301). Unable to cope with these internal conflicts, Virginia resorts to procrastination, tears, and sleep.

"Two Tupenny Ones, Please"

In "Two Tupenny Ones, Please," Mansfield takes a satirical, unusual approach to the "home front" during World War I. As she presents an overheard conversation between two English military women on a train, she demonstrates how people tend to trivialize war and its consequences to society. KM experiments with point of view in this story. Although the narrator's identity remains a mystery, Mansfield's uncommon technique falls easily into the category of limited omniscient. The narrator does not speak, but listens and hears only one of the women; and like the narrator, the reader must infer what the other woman is saying. Thus, as the reader knows only as much as the narrator knows, Mansfield manipulates the reader into anger and indignation at the petty rambling of the two women. Still, a reader can sense the absurdity of war as they talk. KM offers a sketch of the psychological condition of women whose men have left to fight on the continent. She creates irony as the women must maintain the home economy and services while struggling to keep their vain feminine identities.

While clinging to their forgetfulness toward war, the women are vain, self-absorbed, and complacent toward their positions at a military hospital. They gossip about various acquaintances and colleagues, including an officer named Teddy and his wife. To them the tasks of war seem impersonal: the lady speaks with apathy about the officer's wife "notifying the deaths, or finding the missing" (303). To her, even the wife's description of the job as "too depressing for words" has a positive side: her office-mates "make their own tea, and get cakes in turn from Stewart's" (304). The job fades into the background as the woman places more emphasis on the description of teatime than on the reality of war. The lady has her own disquieting role in the war, as she apparently nurses wounded soldiers and "(trots) them out every Tuesday" (304) to entertain them. Yet she speaks with more urgency about when she is free for a game of bridge, placing a bureaucratic distance between her duty and herself.

Yet one can hardly blame the women for their apathy; war disrupts social structures and deprives people of the security of a stable social life. As men leave the women at home to fight on the continent, the women must turn to their own devices to find amusement and a semblance of stability. They must adjust their coping abilities to match the intensity of war; if they are vain and self-absorbed in peace-time society, they must maintain that vanity in war and increase it proportionally. Ultimately, Mansfield presents characters struggling with identity in the most adverse of human conditions. To maintain sanity—a social standard—in such conditions, one must uphold one's identity even to the point of appearing absurd. To Mansfield those vain ways are always intolerable; but these victims of war magnify their defenses like a microscope magnifies wounded tissue.

"A Suburban Fairy Tale"

Mansfield's "A Suburban Fairy Tale" is a very different kind of fairy tale told about a seemingly everyday suburban family. This tale is set against the background of what starts out as a very typical suburbanite breakfast with Mr. B, Mrs. B, and Little B all gathered around the dining table. This family seems to be what Mansfield would consider quite typical in that the father is a self-centered, egotistical man, the woman is the "preening" type with seemingly little or no personality, and both of them spend most of their time ignoring their child, who, of course, cannot ever live up to the expectations they have of him. The main character would seem at first to be Mr. B because KM introduces him first and gives the reader a view into his thoughts. However, later on we see that this view of Mr. B simply underlines his egotistical nature, and the main character is really the ignored, almost invisible Little B. The description of Little B helps to create fairy-tale feeling that Mansfield is striving for. He is a slight little thing with "big wide-open eyes." He reminds one a bit of Lawrence's Paul in "The Rocking-Horse Winner." Little B is endeared to the reader because he is so small in such a big, hostile world. We read that "Mrs. B loved him as only weak children are loved" (311), and that does seem to encompass the feelings she and her husband must have for Little B. However, that is as far as their love will take them. They do not ever listen to the child, and he lives in a quite lonely world among two parents who talk over him of housekeeping matters such as what to have for dinner. In fact, food seems to be a focal point for the B's. And they are so busy making sure that Little B gets enough to eat that they forget to give him "nourishment" in the form of real attention and love.

The conflict in the story, then, lies with the difference between the kind and amount of love that Mr. and Mrs. B can give to their child and the great amount of love that he needs. This conflict is paralleled with the needs of the hungry sparrows outside. It makes sense, then, that Little B is the only one that hears the sparrows and sympathizes with them. The parallel is made clearer when the sparrows turn into little boys; their cries for food parallel Little B's cries for love. Not surprisingly, it takes his parents a while, indicated by the spacing in the text, to realize that Little B is missing and has joined the sparrows/boys outside. The fairy tale feeling is carried further when the reader questions how Little B got outside and how he saw the birds in the first place through the closed curtains. From the start, the child seems to have some story-book kind of connection with the sparrows.

Joining with the sparrows and flying away does not really resolve the conflict; after all, the sparrows are still hungry, crying "Want something to eat, want something to eat" (313). But the conflict does at least seem resolved in a way that a fairy tale is often resolved. The evil, self-centered parents are punished for their sins because their son is taken away from them. And Little B is at least not alone now that he has joined other little lonely children, the hungry sparrows.

"This Flower"

The narrator of "This Flower" is undergoing a medical examination by a doctor of questionable reputation, and although her condition is never named, details—the need for secrecy and recurring floral imagery—indicate that she is pregnant. She, who remains unnamed, receives the news, and although it appears to be bad news, she has a moment of total acceptance which she calls "her moment." Roy, her lover, claims before the examination that he wouldn't mind people knowing if she is pregnant; however, he seeks an unknown doctor who he expects to be discreet, and afterwards, unaware that she is pregnant, says "it would have been so—fatal—so fatal!" (408).

Flowers, the reproductive organs of plants which symbolize life and fertility, appear in the title, the Bloomsbury address of the doctor and the bouquet of anemones, but the introductory quotation, the narrator's feeling of fighting against the stream of life, and Roy's exclamation of fatality undercut life images with death images. Mansfield also uses this story of pregnancy to explore deception and power in male-female relationships. The couple deceive society by choosing a discreet doctor, and the narrator deceives Roy by telling him that she only needs a bit of rest. At first the couple seem to be working together, but Roy whose name—Roy King—suggests dominance controls the situation. He chooses the doctor, discusses feeding the narrator as if she were a child, and may be the only one who does not want the pregnancy.

Once again, Mansfield attacked men by creating a male character who is outwardly loving but insensitive to the needs of the woman in his life. He refers to the possibility of pregnancy as "what neither of us want it to be" (406), yet the narrator never says that she does not wish to be pregnant. The reader must figure out what is happening in the story from details, often ambiguous or incomplete, which are revealed by the characters rather than from a complete, explanatory narrative; consequently, the story is revealed rather than told. Mansfield provides as many questions as answers, and forces the reader to become actively engaged in the story.

"The Wrong House"

"The Wrong House" is a story of mistaken identity. Mrs. Bean, the central character, is sitting and knitting a vest for some needy children when a funeral procession comes up the street. Mrs. Bean thinks it odd that Dollicas, her house maid, hasn't remarked who it is that has died. When the procession stops in front of her house, Mrs. Bean is gripped by terror. The men find it strange that the blinds aren't down at this house, as was the custom at the residence of someone who had died. The men come up and knock at the door. Mrs. Bean mutters that they have gotten the wrong house. The men apologize and leave. Then Dollicas returns. The incident so frightens Mrs. Bean that she can no longer knit, and Dollicas thinks that Mrs. Bean has simply been sleeping.

The central character in this short story is Mrs. Bean. Mansfield doesn't give much information about Mrs. Bean. It is left to the reader to infer that Mrs. Bean is a widow since her husband is never mentioned, and in many ways Mrs. Bean is the epitome of the stereotypical widow. She knits all day, and finds supreme importance in the most mundane aspects of daily life. When she remarks that Dollicas is shopping slower, the reader can see the two have been together a long time. The reader also gets the impression that Mrs. Bean has a very regimented routine which she follows everyday. However, the day the funeral procession comes very much upsets Mrs. Bean's routine. It upsets her so much she can no longer function.

The central conflict in this story occurs within the mind of Mrs. Bean. One can only surmise that the extreme terror which grips Mrs. Bean has a very real source. For most people, someone mistaking their house would be no real crisis. For Mrs. Bean, the terror captivates her and renders her helpless. Mansfield does not give the reason for this phobia. Mansfield writes, "It was as if she had fallen into a cave whose walls were darkness" (410). Perhaps the hearse reminds her of her husband's death; perhaps it reminds her of her own mortality. After the incident, Mrs. Bean unravels the part of the vest she had been knitting. With this action, it is as if Mrs. Bean wants to destroy anything which would remind her of that particularly terror-filled moment in time. The story ends with Dollicas returning to prepare the evening meal. Mrs. Bean realizes that she doesn't have very long left to live. The final sentence of the story is rather disturbing, and reinforces Mrs. Bean's terror: "...Dollicas understood and answered, 'It's a lovely young bird!' as she *pulled down the blind* before going back to the kitchen..." (411).

Chapter Eight
Conclusion:
KM and Other Contemporary
British Short Story Writers

This concluding chapter compares Mansfield to some other short story writers. Rather than proffering generalizations and value judgments about Mansfield and a bunch of other writers, this chapter makes some conclusions by pointing to specific stories both by Mansfield and other writers. Precision, rather than generalization, is the aim in this chapter, as is the aim in all preceding chapters.

Elizabeth Bowen

As Katherine Mansfield finds a deep social concern in the Britain of World War I and shortly before, Elizabeth Bowen develops short, poignant sketches of a London under siege in World War II. As Angus Wilson emphasizes in his introduction to Bowen's *Collected Stories*, Bowen recalls the terror of a society shaking apart during the *Blitzkrieg*. If "Germans at Meat" offers an allegory for the growing social conflicts between countries in pre-Great War Europe, "Breakfast" presents a chronicle of one man's sense of captivity in an environment swooning under trauma and struggling to maintain its unity.

The vehicle in each story is the same: the English narrator of "Germans at Meat" feels more intimidated as the German appetite for lunch grows more voracious and the insults to England become more hostile; likewise, Mr. Rossiter finds breakfast less tolerable as the residents of his mostly female boarding-house "family" attack each other in turns until they reach a consensus on one-point—how best to cope with a national transportation strike. Thus, each author presents a setting that best demonstrates the nature of social groups in conflict; when the characters gather for

135

meals, what should be the most sociable time of day becomes a stressful point for hostilities and fears to surface. Furthermore, each author successfully uses sexual conflict as a metaphor for growing social chasms: at the end of Mansfield's story, when the Germans demand their meals, the narrator retreats as if threatened sexually; likewise, when Mr. Rossiter feels pressure to choose one of the woman in his house as a wife, he cringes at the notion of further confinement to his uneasy existence with a hostile family.

Here lies a difference, however. While Bowen chooses a more personal, familial setting for this conflict, Mansfield places her narrator in a more distant relation with the other characters, and with a powerful effect. Not only does the narrator feel inept in her attempt to get along with the Germans; she must cope with their especially arrogant manners and displays of virility. When she retreats, she feels intimidated and ostracized like a young girl in a clubhouse for boys. The sexual advance that the German appetite represents is not the kind that arises from affection, but from a demand for control, without regard for the individual; and the narrator can only retreat for fear that the German virility and increasing hostility will turn into rape. Indeed, the narrator's weakness represents Britain's weakness at the time. Like Britain, she neither wants nor expects the Germans' advance, and she is not prepared to defend herself against their violent onslaught. She must leave as quietly as possible and continue her own cultural identity as best she can despite German invasion. Thus Mansfield's allegory is a prediction, perhaps a warning drill for the condition of life that Bowen's allegory later depicts.

While KM draws a conflict between two societies on the eve of war, Bowen isolates a family within a society suffering the consequences of war. While Bowen offers no mention of World War II, the family's condition parallels the conditions of Britain during the *Blitzkrieg*. As the members of this artificial family quibble over vain, frivolous issues, the British economy is in shambles. By story's end, Jervis Bevel, who has been perusing a newspaper as if holding a barricade, reveals that "another" railway strike is about to begin, and the family members must unite under some agreement about how to deal with the strike. The family deals with the railway strike like it would an "air" strike—it decides on the best train to take on the decreased schedule and scrambles to catch the train as if running to the cellar. The family is an assembly of unlikely housemates waiting for better times; everyone seems out to gain something from everyone else's ego, with hidden hostilities mounting as in a parliament struggling against its own dissent. Mr. Rossiter punctuates the family's condition as he dreads entering the breakfast room: "Behold, I die daily."

What "dies" is his hope. He feels trapped in a cycle of conflict, a coexistence based on necessity, as a boarding house provides an economically efficient system. He fears the pressure to marry, as marriage would seal him in his despair over the endless quibbling. Yet as he dreads his daily existence, he perceives the need for the conciliatory elements—particularly for Mrs. Russel, the housekeeper who, while contributing to the monotony of egotism, nevertheless provides a needed sense of order. At least Mrs. Russel protects the family from a "rushed breakfast." Thus, like Mansfield's narrator who escapes the German onslaught only temporarily, Mr. Rossiter would like to escape the system, but cannot. For both authors the coming of war is the death of hope, a suspension of livelihood. They can attempt to avoid the harsh reality by retreating from it or building defenses, but, as in death and war, they must face the terror of circumstances beyond their control or foresight. Despite their struggle to maintain unity, the characters of both stories feel isolated and helpless, wounded by their futile efforts at being themselves.

Anton Chekhov

Katherine Mansfield and Anton Chekhov are two principal figures to examine when tracing the development of the story as a genre. That Mansfield held Chekhov in high regard is well established, but one might ask the reasons behind Mansfield's intense admiration, almost deification, of Chekhov. Chekhov had accomplished two tasks of which Mansfield was envious. He had introduced Russian literature, and in it pictures of Russian life, to the world, and he had furthered the development of the short story as a form of art. Mansfield, having a fierce love for her homeland, New Zealand, felt "it was her duty, her object, and her achievement to do the same for her 'undiscovered country' as Chekhov helped to do for Mother Russia" (Alpers 322-23). The two also share a common view of what the artist's task is. Mansfield writes, "What the writer does is not so much *to solve* the question but *to put* the question" (Hanson 34).

Since both writers operate within the genre of short fiction, they also share areas of commonality and similarities of technique, and it is in these similarities where Chekhov's influence on Mansfield is most strongly felt. These similarities are: "their choosing for their themes and the study of the life of the soul, their aptitude for creation of atmosphere, (and) their technique for using daydreams for the revelations of the minds of the characters" (Friis 157-58). Hanson also notes that, for each author, "Action is less important than atmosphere and...the process of language tends increasingly to become part of the subject as well as the agent of composition" (Hanson 16-17). All of these stylistics exist because the authors possess similar attitudes toward life.

It could be effectively argued that both Mansfield and Chekhov have somewhat bleak and dreary views of life. Many of their characters are oppressed, trapped in a solitary and meaningless existence in which there is no hope. Both authors were sick for the latter part of their lives, and their pessimism is evidenced in the texts they created. Alpers notes that "There was a deceptively close resemblance between the two writers' views of life, and hence between the forms they evolved to express them" (Alpers 214). By examining the recurrent theme of the mystery of life and death and the portrayal of class differences in Mansfield's "The Life of Ma Parker" and Chekov's "Misery," one can see how strikingly similar the two views of society and life held by the two authors really are.

The subject of death, and how it related to the cycle of life, was always a principle concern for Katherine Mansfield. In her stories such as "The Fly," "The Voyage," and "The Life of Ma Parker," the subject of death plays a major role. In examining "essential characteristics" of a Katherine Mansfield story, Alpers notes that Mansfield "isolate(s) one cry from the heart to make it represent the whole of a human problem" (Alpers 131). The way a character deals with death is critical for Mansfield. As her health began to decline, Mansfield focuses increasingly on the "mystery" of death. "The mystery of life and death...timeless and universal...was absorbing KM more and more as she approached the peak of her achievement" (Alpers 323). "The Life of Ma Parker" was published in 1920, three years before KM's death. In the story, Ma Parker's grandson, Lennie, has recently died. The story is developed as a psychological sequence. Ma Parker goes back and forth between her memories of Lennie while he was still living and the effect his death has had on her. His death has caused her to be totally alone in the world, and she can find neither someone to talk to nor a place in which she can vent her emotion. Mansfield makes the reader sympathize with Ma's utter isolation.

This isolation is also felt for Iona, Chekhov's principal character in "Misery." Iona, a cabby, has recently buried his only son. He, too, cannot find anyone to listen to his story. Although he has a living daughter, his son's death has caused him an incredible amount of sorrow. Chekhov, like Mansfield, makes the reader feel the sense of loss experienced by Iona. This sense of loss is most poignantly demonstrated when the only sympathetic ear Iona finds belongs to his horse. In a letter to William Gerhardi, Mansfield writes that she uses death to show "the diversity of life and how we try to fit in everything. Death included" (Magalaner 110). Both authors show a certain affinity for the subject of death, but they treat death as simply a part of life. Another area of life which is explored by both authors is social stratification, and how this stratification affects the members of society.

In a comparison of Chekhov and Mansfield, Marvin Magalaner notes that both authors are "concerned with the middle class as it provides ammunition for social satire" (Magalaner 22-23). In "The Life of Ma Parker" and "Misery," the middle class is shown to be viciously self-centered and unconcerned about the lower classes. By using both actual, physical description and conversation written in dialect, KM and Chekhov show the disparity of the classes in each story. In "The Life of Ma Parker" Ma "bent her head and hobbled off to the kitchen, clasping the old fish bag that held her cleaning things and an apron and a pair of felt shoes" (Mansfield 141). No one cares for this poor, old woman. The only function she serves to the "literary gentlemen" is to cook his meals, to clean his house, and to carry out his garbage. When the gentleman asks Ma about her grandson's death, the reader can readily infer that he doesn't really care how Ma feels; rather, he asked her in order to make conversation.

By making Ma's speech full of double negatives and other non-standard dialectal variations, Mansfield demonstrates Ma's position in the social hierarchy. Mansfield shows that people of the middle class do not have even a shred of human decency left; however, her indictment of the middle class is not nearly as vicious as Chekhov's. In "Misery" the members of the middle class are abusive, both verbally and physically, to Iona. Again, he simply lives in order to serve those who both oppress and abuse him. When he pleadingly asks his riders to briefly listen to his problems, they consciously ignore his request. The sense of frustration the reader feels for Iona is also present in "The Life of Ma Parker," and in other works by both authors.

Frustration is also an element which figures into the short fiction of Katherine Mansfield and Anton Chekhov. Friis notes that "In their stories, KM and Chekhov adhere to a grim realism, which makes the stories generally end on a note of frustration" (Friis 158n). I believe frustration is a key element which unites both Mansfield and Chekhov. Chekhov, just as Mansfield, felt frustration as he became sicker because he wanted to accomplish much more, but, at the end of his life, Chekhov gave up hope. Mansfield wrote, "There is no more Chekhov. Illness has swallowed him" (Alpers 349). Mansfield never really gave up hope, although she did finally succumb to her illness. Both Mansfield and Chekhov were frustrated with the literature which had been written before them. They felt an incredible need to break new ground in literature, and they did. The "grim realism" displayed in almost all of their stories reflects the life of each artist. Both Mansfield and Chekhov knew that life does not always follow a perfect course, and the authors present this idea in their works. Their frustration stemmed from knowing that they could accomplish greater things, but they also knew that their lives were going to be cut short. A certain sense of frustration is found in any artist, in anyone who can truly create, but harnessing the power of this frustration and using it to create such works of art is only possible in the caliber of artist such as Katherine Mansfield or Anton Chekhov.

James Joyce

James Joyce and Katherine Mansfield share many artistic likenesses in their approaches and techniques in short story writing. Although the two authors were acquainted with one another, there is no evidence or knowledge that proves one author was influenced by the other. According to Maria Gottwald, Mansfield admired *A Portrait of the Artist as a Young Man*, while she found *Ulysses*, to be puzzling and bewildering (Gottwald 41). It is not unique that Mansfield was affected in this way by *Ulysses*, for most, if not all, of Joyce's writing as well as her own writing is difficult to read, to interpret, and to understand by the most attentive reader. Gottwald is convinced that Joyce and Mansfield share at least two very important attitudes.

First, a vigorous sense of independence, which is also reflected in their writing by the pervading themes of loneliness and alienation; secondly, an unflinching dedication to art coupled with rigorous inward discipline—to both writers art was a vocation rather than a career, both were conscious...deliberate experimenters and innovators. (Gottwald 41)

The objective of this section is to examine some of the approaches and techniques of short story writing James Joyce and Katherine Mansfield employed. More specifically, plot struture will be illustrated using openings and closings in "Grace" and "Bliss."

Joyce and Mansfield often forego the pattern we refer to as traditional plot development: chronological sequence, with an elaborate exposition; plot movement rising to a climax and conclusion (Gottwald 42). Joyce's "Grace" exemplifies a non-traditional approach. The story opens precipitously, lacking introductory or preparatory explanation.

Two gentlemen who were in the lavatory at the time tried to lift him up: but he was quite helpless. He lay curled up at the foot of the stairs down which he had fallen. They succeeded in turning him over. His hat had rolled a few yards away and his clothes were smeared with the filth and ooze of the floor on which he had lain, face downwards. His eyes were closed and he breathed with a grunting noise. A thin stream of blood trickled from the corner of his mouth. (Joyce 150)

Joyce often begins his short stories in the middle of the action. This technique truly captures the attention of a reader. No reader can assume Joyce's intentions based on an opening. All that is known based on this particular opening is a man's condition. What we do not know is the extenuating circumstance that brought on this helpless condition. It is several paragraphs later before the reader is made aware of the individual's name. Further, it is much later in the story that one realizes the very first sentence actually foreshadows the whole story.

Mansfield's openings are similar in technique. She, too, dispenses with elaborate expository openings. The following opening paragraph is taken from "Bliss."

Although Bertha Young was thirty she still had moments like this when she wanted to run instead of walk, to take dancing steps on and off the pavement, to bowl a hoop, to throw something up in the air and catch it again, or to stand still and laugh at—nothing—at nothing, simply. (377)

Although Mansfield provides the reader with the name and age, this story still begins in the middle of the action. The reader does not know very much, if anything at all, about Bertha Young or why she is feeling so excited. Again, this is enough to capture attention; the excited anticipation engages one's interest to continue reading. Gottwald concludes that many stories written by Joyce and Mansfield "open *in medias res*...before some climactic event, commonplace enough by itself yet significant for the characters' inner experience..." (Gottwald 175). For instance, in "Grace" the inner experience is related to the fall and uncertain redemption of the central figure, Tom Kernan; in "Bliss" the inner experience is related to Bertha's acceptance that her bliss is only an illusion, for her husband is having an affair with Pearl Fulton.

Joyce and Mansfield tend to end their stories as abruptly as they open. According to Gottwald, "open endings are...more pronounced with Joyce than with Mansfield" (43). In "Grace" Joyce provides the reader with a detailed account of Tom Kernan on the filthy lavatory floor at the bottom of the stairs; there is a detailed account of his friends at his bedside, who are supposedly concerned with his spiritual welfare; finally, there is the retreat, which takes place at the Gardiner Street Church, Father Purdon presiding. The following is Father Purdon's final message delivered to "businesslike men" in a "businesslike way"

—Well, I have verified my accounts. I find all well. But if, as might happen, there were some discrepancies, to admit the truth, to be frank and say like a man:—Well, I have looked into my accounts. I find this wrong and this wrong. But, with God's grace, I will rectify this and this. I will set right my accounts. (Joyce 174)

Although Joyce reports with detail Father Purdon's message, the reader is still not sure where speculation should end. What next? is a common question asked by Joyce's readers; however, even in the end, Tom Kernan's redemption still remains uncertain. Moreover, it must be remembered that this technique is designed in many ways to permit an ambiguous response.

In "Bliss" Mansfield provides the reader with a detailed account of the conflicting emotion and narration of Bertha Young. Although Bertha insists that her excitement during the day (while planning a dinner party) is blissful, it is really an attempt repeatedly to deceive herself, for she knows that her husband is having an affair with her newly-found friend, Pearl Fulton. Mansfield's concluding lines are

Bertha simply ran over to the long windows. "Oh, what is going to happen now?" she cried. But the pear tree was as lovely as ever and as full of flower and as still. (350)

The pear tree in this case symbolizes life in full bloom. The rhetorical question remains "...what is going to happen now?" (350). Again, where does the speculation for the reader end? The serious Joyce and Mansfield reader learns to appreciate and to comprehend the techniques these modern artists employed, and regardless of their techniques, the reader, who puts forth a concerted effort to understand these artists, will be rewarded by feeling a sense of completeness.

D.H. Lawrence

In many of their respective short stories, both D.H. Lawrence and Katherine Mansfield explore themes of focussing on the relationship between men and women. While their perspectives differ dramatically, sharing neither stylistic qualities nor social points of view, they both provide insight into the nature of these relationships. Both suggest that the success of male/female involvements depends to a large extent on the woman's self-effacement or self-falsification. This section will explore the treatment that this theme receives in a sampling of short stories by both authors.

D.H. Lawrence, in two of his short stories, "The Borderline" and "The Overtone," explores the aforementioned theme. In each story the success of the male/female relationship depends on the woman's suppression of her identity and her decision to submit to the man's will. Clearly Lawrence feels that self-effacement is a woman's nature, and that her true will dictates that she should function in this manner without question. In "The Borderline" the central female character is Katherine Farquhar, a young woman recently widowed and re-married. Katherine, an initially strong, rather independent woman with a clear sense of her own identity, now married to what she regards as a somewhat ineffectual man, unhappily looks back on her previous relationship with longing and regret, wondering why she is dissatisfied currently. While married to her first husband she recalls feeling stifled, without place, always having to defend her "self." She says of her first marital relationship—"they were both too proud and unforgiving to yield to one another" (Lawrence 589). They were always involved in a battle of wills. She describes her former husband as "unyielding and haughty" (Lawrence 589). Her current husband envyingly describes him as "the only real man (he) ever knew" (Lawrence 590). Yet the first husband was cruel, relentless in his efforts to triumph and break Katherine's will—forcing her to submit to him. He had no regard for her as an individual, whatsoever. She recalls telling him—"You don't even know that a woman exists" (Lawrence 589). In spite of his treatment of her, Lawrence heralds him as the ideal male.

Now that Katherine is in a relationship with Phillip, a man who treats her at least as an individual with her own identity, she, oddly enough, wishes she were living her old life again—ironically, a life of repression. While on a midnight vigil, Katherine encounters her dead husband who supernaturally reveals to her the problem of their past relationship and her present unhappiness. He explains to her that the failure of their relationship resulted from her refusal to submit to him and efface her identity. She now recognizes, after their encounter, that "no matter what the man does or is, as a person...(she should) move at his side in a dim, full flood of contentment" (Lawrence 597). She must "ask no questions of him, but be humble and beyond tears grateful" (Lawrence 597). She realizes that the ultimate in female identity is "the restful, thoughtless pleasure of a woman who moves in the aura of the man to whom she belongs" (Lawrence 596). Hence, Lawrence seems to advocate female self-effacement as the solution to the problems of male/female relationships. In order to gratify the male ego and to satisfy her own supposed natural impulses of submission, the woman must unquestioningly give herself up to the man's will and all will be well (at least for the man).

In "The Overtone" Lawrence deals with the same theme. Mr. and Mrs. Renshaw, a married couple of several years, appear to be "good friends. It was said that they were the most friendly couple in the county. And that was it" (Lawrence 754). But, in reality they detest each other. They were at one time happy, but because Mrs. Renshaw failed to submit to her husband's wishes and refused to make love to him one evening in the meadow, he began to hate her. Once she denied him, asserted her own identity, it was over. Now they live in a loveless marriage, without desire or feeling because of the web of convention that binds them. She, at one time, felt he "was the sun, shining full on her heart when he came to her" (Lawrence 753). But, because she asserted herself, he "ceased to come to her" (Lawrence 753). And she began to hate him and he her. "Everything was essentially over for both of them; they lived on the surface" (Lawrence 752). He now lives his life driving motor cars, bathing wherever he likes. She lives hers meeting with other women, speaking about the suffragist movement.

She feels like a "dumb singer, with the voice of a nightingale yet making discord" (Lawrence 755). He feels like a "castrated bear" (Lawrence 752). They both live and suffer together perpetually, each waiting for a release from their misery, knowing this release will never come because he will not forgive her for the wrong he believes she has committed against him, and she will never submit to him. And all of this because she asked for a choice—a choice she should have been free to make. But, Renshaw robbed her of her freedom, her choice, her life—because of a moment of self assertion. Once again, Lawrence seems to suggest that a woman's submission is the only means of attaining a successful love relationship with a man. That, in fact, she should willingly submit and enjoy it because it is her nature to do so. In these stories, Lawrence does not present the woman as a separate entity with her own unique identity. He merely presents her as a creature designed to be the reflections of a man's desire. The male does not take into account that he is requiring her to play a role— to act out a part—to efface herself. He thinks it is her nature to be this way. In his view, anything less than submission is unnatural. Lawrence is not interested in the effects this might have on the woman. He is simply interested in the effects it has on the man if she refuses to do it.

Katherine Mansfield in "Bliss" and "All Serene" explores the effects that required self-falsification have on the female. She shows us that the woman, after relinquishing her identity for the sake of the relationship with a man, must live out her life without a sense of self, of what she wants or who she is. Instead, she must adapt roles to suit her husband and her society, and practice deception in order merely to survive. Mansfield, unlike Lawrence, feels that it is not a woman's nature to submit, to efface herself; but, she is instead forced to do so by society. For instance, in "Bliss," Bertha and Harry Young appear to be the "perfect" couple. But the only reason is because Bertha pretends to be happy. In fact Bertha lives in the role she is confined to, in a loveless marriage, and feels "shut up in a case like a rare, rare fiddle" (338). She desires more from life—an identity, a relationship with feeling, a sense of her "self," but is trapped by convention and by the prescribed role she has been forced into as wife/mother. She fantasizes about a life of beauty and meaning. She seeks the possibility of true expression.

But Bertha is stuck in a life of concerns about the correct, socially acceptable existence. She has all the "right" friends, the "right" house, the "right" husband—but, she is trapped and can never express her true feelings to anyone. She can never remove her mask. Hence, she must live, confined to her role—longing for more—but never attaining it. Similarly, in "All Serene" the Rutherfords are another supposedly "perfect" couple, but Mona Rutherford, like Bertha, is a consummate actress. She plays the lead role of the perfection of the love she and her husband share. She has made it her duty to create this illusion—"She thought it part of her duty to him—to their love, even, to wear charming little caps, funny little coats...and to see that the table was as perfect as he and she—fastidious pair!" (653). Mona does eventually realize that she has completely lost her identity—her "self"—and has become a mere persona. But, by the time she reaches this conclusion, she can do nothing to change it. Her role is fixed and she cannot give it up. She no longer has an identity to regain. She has become a blind, identityless creature inhabiting a role.

Through this comparison, it becomes clear that male/female relationships do, in fact, work, but only if the woman is willing to falsify herself. Lawrence explores what occurs when the woman fails to efface herself—the relationship fails. Mansfield explores what occurs when the woman succeeds in effacing herself—the relationship succeeds. Both authors, in their different styles and with different sympathies, show that the most crucial element in love relationships between men and women is deception. Deception is easier than loneliness, so relationships persist in spite of this requirement.

Jean Rhys

The modernist period in literature is the time when women authors and women's literature began to bloom. With the turn of the century, there came a change in the way women viewed themselves and their aspirations. No longer content to stay at home and raise a family, women began forging new lives for themselves and dealt with the attendant problems of such a life of their own. Two women who chronicled the problems and hopes and desires of this generation were Katherine Mansfield and Jean Rhys. Both women rejected middle-class marriage for a life of bohemian uncertainty, yet their rewards for this life are a body of work each woman can be proud of, and a place for herself in lliterary history. Katherine Mansfield was born in Wellington, New Zealand in 1888. Her family was well-off, and Mansfield's English education helped her realize that to be the kind of writer she wanted to be, she must leave New Zealand. Although her life was never settled after she left home, Mansfield always managed to keep writing, and she published three volumes of collected stories during her brief lifetime.

Jean Rhys was born in Roseau, Dominica, in the West Indies in 1894. Her father was a doctor who emigrated from Wales and married a girl from a local Creole family. Rhys came to London in 1910, a few years after Mansfield returned from New Zealand, to study at the Royal Academy of Dramatic Art, but her father was not as wealthy as Mansfield's, and she was forced to drop out when he died. Rhys worked as a chorus girl for a time, and in 1919 she married Jean Langlet and moved to the Continent. It was during her marriage to Langlet, especially when she lived in Paris, that she began to write the stories which would appear in *The Left Bank and Other Stories*, published in 1927. This section compares the lives and works of Katherine Mansfield and Jean Rhys, concentrating first on the major themes each woman used in her writing, and then comparing Mansfield's "Feuille d'Album" to Rhys' "Mannequin" and "The Woman at the Store" to "Pioneers, Oh Pioneers."

Mansfield's and Rhys' backgrounds are similar. This similarity extends to the themes they chose to explore in their short stories. Both women came from island nations dependent on Britain and grew up considering that country "home." Each came to London to fulfill her dreams, Mansfield to be a writer, and Rhys at first to be an actress. Mansfield and Rhys also discovered the difficulties that accompany the life of a young colonial woman on her own; the struggle for acceptance in an alien society, monetary problems, and the search for love while trying to maintain the space and time to do her real work, that of an artist. Yet there are also many dissimilarities between the two women. Rhys never suffered Mansfield's bad health; Rhys gave birth to a child in 1922; and she started writing much later than Mansfield, turning to the novel in 1928 with *Quartet*, and writing four more novels and short stories before her death in 1979. Mansfield and Rhys were honest writers, sometimes brutally so, and their short stories are unflinching looks at the lives of those who do not quite fit into society, women mostly, and some men, who feel trapped and isolated, who are the victims of society, but who still struggle to make some meaning out of an existence they don't quite understand. As colonials, these authors were also interested in their home countries, and how growing up on a small island shapes responses to the world. What both women were striving to put down on paper was the truth as they saw it, in order to strike a responsive chord in their readers.

Mansfield and Rhys both lived in Paris for a time, although Mansfield was less settled than Rhys, who stayed for a longer period because her husband was jailed for a year on art fraud charges. Mansfield was in and out of the city, and she set only a small number of stories there, compared to those set in London and New Zealand. Rhys, however, set all of her first collection of stories in Paris, specifically the Left Bank, which in the years following the First World War was more of a state of mind than a place. Mansfield is not considered by some critics to be a part of the literary Left Bank group, and Rhys as well was "an outsider among outsiders, neither part of the cafe crowd nor an occasional visitor to Sylvia Beach's bookshop" (Benstock 448).

This condition of alienation is reflected in Mansfield's "Feuille d'Album" and Rhys' "Mannequin," both set in Paris. "Feuille d'Album" concerns a young artist, Ian French, who appears to be the perfect Parisian artist type: "He had black close-cropped hair, grey eyes with long lashes, white cheeks and a mouth pouting as though he were determined not to cry...How could one resist him?" (109). Yet French turns out to be quite resistible, even "hopeless" when he refuses to respond to the cafe women's kind ministrations. He lives in a dreamworld of his own, fixing his sights on the young woman who lives opposite, constructing from glimpses of her through her balcony what their life would be like. French determines that he will get to know this girl, who seems to be his perfect soulmate, and follows her one day as she does her shopping. Although he agonizes over speaking to her, he lets the girl get all the way to the door before he brusquely hands her an egg she has dropped.

In "Mannequin," another Parisian type, a fashioned-house model, begins her first job in the industry. Anna is eager to join what seems to be the elegant world of the mannequin, but she soon discovers that elegance is only a show. Behind the glittering salon is a warren of drab and dingy rooms; the mannequins themselves are more like their types, the *gamine*, and *Femme fatale*, than real people and the work itself is boring and tiresome, for Anna stands on her feet all day being poked and prodded by various buyers. Yet at the end of the day, a certain satisfaction Anna feels with her work gives rise to her feeling that now she is a true Parisian and causes her to smile as she watches the other mannequins leaving the shops up and down the boulevard. Both of these stories are small slices of Parisian life, told from the point of view of two innocents who seem to be a bit bewildered and isolated from their surroundings. The romanticism of Paris is something they want to believe in, but ironically, the ugliness of reality is always hidden just below the surface.

"The Woman at the Store" is one of Mansfield's earliest stories set in New Zealand, and it compares to Rhys's "Pioneers, Oh Pioneers" because both stories are about the effect living in isolation can have on those who are used to civilization. From their vantage points in Europe, Mansfield and Rhys, looking back on their homelands, see that life in a tiny island nation takes certain sacrifices, and that the deep bush or rainforest can be an unforgiving place for those who are not fit to make those sacrifices. "The Woman at the Store" is a story about three travelers in the New Zealand bush who come upon a woman and her daughter running a makeshift store. One of the travelers remembers the place from a few years ago, when the woman was pretty and her husband was friendly and generous. Now the woman is frazzled, her looks gone, as well as her husband, who is away "shearing." She and her daughter seem glad to have some company at their isolated outpost and treat their visitors to supper. Neither the mother nor the daughter seems too stable from their extended stay in the bush. The mother pours out her tale of woe to the visitors and does her best to flirt with one of them, while the daughter communicates mostly through pictures. During the night, the daughter reveals through a picture the terrible secret of the place: her mother shot her father and buried him. Next morning, two of the travelers leave with a promise from the third: "I'll pick you up later" (449).

"Pioneers, Oh Pioneers" is also a murder mystery set in the isolated rainforests of Dominica. The story is a story within a story, focussing first on two sisters aged 11 and nine, who know that some people on the island are considered "crazy," including Mr. Ramage, whom the story concerns, but one sister, Rosalie, has a schoolgirl crush on him. The story then focuses on their father's acquaintance with Ramage, and Ramage's slow decline from a proper, though rather anti-social English gentleman, to the wildman of the jungle, who tramps around naked or lies in his hammock all day. Ramage came to Dominica looking for peace, but when he married a black woman he scandalized both the whites and blacks of the island. His strange behavior leads the local newspaper to accuse him of murder when his wife disappears, and the angry blacks of the island stone his house and threaten to burn him out. A delegations of whites comes to speak to Ramage after a near riot the night before, but Ramage has committed suicide needlessly, for his wife had only run away from him. Most of the white islanders are relieved to be rid of an embarrassing nuisance, but Rosalie is heart-broken. Both stories are presented in a candid way, making no apologies for the different morality which rules in the isolated areas of the world. New Zealand and Dominica, though they import English people and English customs, still are not small slices of England, but wild, primitive lands where English law becomes senseless.

Mansfield and Rhys have much in common as these two stories demonstrate. It is when their work is examined in totality, however, that their differences emerge. Mansfield writes in a different spirit from Rhys. KM is not so defeated, more ironic, more defiant, and more enthralled with the spirit of life than is Rhys. Rhys's heroines are mostly sad, slightly seedy women who are used and abused by the world with no way to defend themselves. Falling in love for them is akin to letting down one's defenses to let the enemy rush in, for the men in her works are always the ones with the power. Mansfield, although she is not naive about relationships, refuses to concede power to the men in her stories. Mansfield is also more interested in a character's inner life than is Rhys, about the way subjective feelings can affect a person's outlook. But comparing the world of these two women is fruitful because each helps to illuminate the work of the other by examining similar themes in a different light.

Virginia Woolf

Months before meeting her, Virginia Woolf wrote, "Katherine Mansfield has dogged my steps for three years" (Tomalin 157).

And in the summer of 1917, these two extraordinary women finally met, beginning a very important friendship that would last, on again and off again, until Mansfield's death in 1923. Each woman left a lasting impression on the other, seeming to bring out the best and the worst in each other. Bonded by common goals, theirs was truly a unique relationship; "Never again shall I have one like it," Virginia once stated (Tomalin 204). However special this relationship was, it was still a fragile one, subject to the ferocity of Bloomsbury gossip, and to the petty jealousies that each woman held for the other. Both of these women, it seems, were enslaved by incredible insecurities, and each of them had had to fight as women in a man's world. These factors combined to make it very difficult for either of them to develop true friendships with peers. Underneath this fragility, however, there seems to have been something stronger, a bond that held them together. "Yet," Virginia wrote, "I still feel, somehow that friendship persists...For our friendship was a real thing we said..." (Tomalin 203).

When Katherine met Virginia at the Woolfs' home in June of 1917, she met a Virginia that was "secure in her husband and her home, with a room to write in...and no need at all to repudiate her family or feel estranged by being creative" (Alpers 248). She had no idea of Virginia's battles with mental illness, seeing only what she envisioned as a very close to perfect life. Katherine, with her own life full of instabilities, would always be jealous of this. Virginia, on the other hand, "was jealous of what Katherine might attain" (Alpers 260). Katherine's incredible talent disturbed Virginia and called to mind what she considered her own shortcomings. At the time of this meeting Virginia was 34 years old, with one novel behind her. Katherine was 28, and already had met with some success. It is easy to understand why Alpers states, "It was the elder one...who feared that the younger might surpass her" (Alpers 247). Each woman, throughout the course of the friendship, had to battle against her own jealousies for the other. It is interesting to note that the same insecurities that probably helped to bring them together as friends also constantly worked to drive them apart.

The literary relationship that existed between Katherine and Virginia seems to be the strongest bond that they shared. They shared common views about their work, and each placed her role as a writer above all else. Katherine and Virginia were interested in many of the same issues, such as "the ambivalences of family life and feeling between men and women, parents and children" (Tomalin 200). The bond is deeper than this, however.

Virginia found the other expressing her feelings as she had never heard them expressed: to no one but Leonard could she speak in the same disembodied way about writing without altering her thought more than she altered it in her diary. (Alpers 259)

Katherine seemed to feel much the same way about their conversations and feelings about literature, writing in a letter to Virginia,

We have got the same job, Virginia and it is really very curious and thrilling that we should both, quite apart from each other, be after so very nearly the same thing. (Alpers 251)

Though they had very different styles of writing, when Katherine and Virginia got together they expressed the same opinions; further, they each seemed to share the thoughts of the other. Soon after each meeting, "They fell into step" (Alpers 259). Both Virginia and Katherine felt these experiences to be quite phenomenal, and their admiration and respect for each other is obvious.

Because of this admiration and respect, this incredible literary bond they shared, Virginia and Katherine contributed a great deal to each other's work. Virginia was quite instrumental in the writing of Katherine's "Aloe," encouraging her to write it and get it published. This story, later renamed "Prelude," is one of KM's most successful. About it Katherine stated, " 'As far as I know it's more or less my own invention' " (Tomalin 162). "Prelude" was full of original elements, most notably "its setting...and its handling of mood and character" (Tomalin 162). Woolf, on the other hand, was seemingly encouraged by Katherine to write her short story "Kew Gardens." Alpers suggests that the writing of "Kew Gardens" was "at Katherine's direct prompting" (Alpers 251), and we can at least surmise that KM encouraged Virginia in the writing of the story. In a letter to Virginia, Katherine writes,

Your Flower Bed is very good. There's a still, quivering changing light over it all and a sense of those couples dissolving in the bright air which fascinates me. (Alpers 251)

Through at least her encouragement, and possibly through her own directions, Katherine "helped Virginia Woolf to break out of the mold in which she had been working hitherto" (Alpers 252). At times these two women did not agree, and their criticisms of each other were quite damaging, particularly Mansfield's sincere yet debilitating criticism of Woolf's *Night and Day*. However, they helped each other greatly in many ways. Through their mutual encouragement, both Virginia and Katherine benefitted a great deal from their friendship and literary relationship.

But what was it about these two that drew them together yet drove them apart? What mysterious influences were behind their puzzling relationship? At times they seemed intensely drawn to one another, yet soon there would again be "rocks ahead" (Alpers 257). It is true that they disagreed on many issues, and their lifestyles were quite different. However, they also had many things in common. They "faced some of the same problems, such as ill health and childlessness" (Tomalin 205). They also shared the serious burden of incredible insecurity. Tomalin states, "The approach of these two unstable, delicate and extraordinary women to one another was hesitant" (Tomalin 160). Surely these qualities they shared were the very elements that simultaneously created their strong bonds and drove them apart with prejudice and jealousy.

Works Cited

Alpers, Antony. *Katherine Mansfield: A Biography.* New York: Knopf, 1953.

_____. *The Life of Katherine Mansfield.* New York: Viking, 1980.

Bal, Mieke. *Narratology: Introduction to the Theory of Narrative.* Amsterdam, 1980.

Benstock, Shari. *Women of the Left Bank: Paris 1900-1940.* Austin: U of Texas, 1986.

Chatman, Seymour. *Story and Discourse: Narrative Structure in Fiction and Film.* Ithaca, NY: Cornell UP, 1978.

Daly, Saralyn. *Katherine Mansfield.* New York: Twayne, 1965.

Dowling, David, ed. *Katherine Mansfield: Dramatic Sketches.* Palmerston North: Nagare, 1988.

Friis, Anne. *Katherine Mansfield: Life and Stories.* Copenhagen: Munksgaard, 1946.

Gordon, Ian, ed. *The Urewera Notebook.* Oxford: Oxford UP, 1978.

Gottwald, Maria, "New Approaches and Techniques in the Short Story of James Joyce and Katherine Mansfield," *Literary Interrelations: Ireland, England and the World.* Eds. Wolfgang Zach and Henry Kosok, vol 2. Germany: Gunter Narr Verlag Tubingen, 1987.

Hankin, Cherry. Introduction. *Bliss, The Garden Party, The Dove's Nest, Something Childish.* Auckland: Century Hutchinson, 1988.

_____. ed. *Letters Between Katherine Mansfield and John Middleton Murry.* London: Virago, 1988.

Hanson, Clare, ed. *The Critical Writing of Katherine Mansfield.* London: Macmillan, 1986.

Joyce, James. *Dubliners.* New York: Penguin, 1976.

Lawrence, D.H. *The Complete Short Stories of D.H. Lawrence.* London: William Heinemann, Ltd., 1955.

Magalaner, Marvin. *The Fiction of Katherine Mansfield.* Carbondale and Edwardsville: Southern Illinois UP, 1971.

Mansfield, Katherine. *Collected Stories of Katherine Mansfield.* London: Constable, 1966.

_____. *Short Stories of Katherine Mansfield.* New York: Knopf, 1941.

_____. *The Garden Party and Other Stories.* New York: Knopf, 1922.

_____. *The Short Stories of Katherine Mansfield.* New York: Ecco, 1983.

_____. *In A German Pension.* London: Stephen Swift, 1911.

_____. *Bliss and Other Stories.* London: Constable, 1920.

_____. *The Garden Party and Other Stories.* London: Constable, 1922.

_____. *The Dove's Nest and Other Stories.* Ed. J.M. Murry. London: Constable, 1923.

_____. *Something Childish and Other Stories*. Ed. J.M. Murry. London: Constable, 1924.

_____. *The Short Stories of Katherine Mansfield*. New York: Ecco, 1937.

_____. *The Aloe, with Prelude*. Ed. Vincent O'Sullivan. Wellington: Port Nicholson, 1972.

Murry, J.M. *Katherine Mansfield and Other Literary Portraits*. London: Peter Nevill, 1949.

O'Sullivan, Vincent, ed. *The Poems of Katherine Mansfield*. Oxford: Oxford UP, 1989.

Scott, Margaret, ed. "The Unpublished Manuscripts of Katherine Mansfield." *Turnbull Library Record* 3.1 (1970): 4-28; 3.3 (1970) 128-33; 4.1 (1971): 4-20; 5.1 (1972): 19-25; 6.2 (1973): 4-8; 7.1 (1974): 4-14.

Short, M.H. *Language and Literature*. New York: Norton, 1985.

Stead, C.K., ed. *The Letters and Journals of Katherine Mansfield: A Selection*. London: Allen Lane, 1977.

Tomalin, Claire. *Katherine Mansfield: A Secret Life*. New York: Knopf, 1988.

Wilson, Angus. Introduction. *The Collected Stories of Elizabeth Bowen*. New York: Alfred A. Knopf, 1981.

Wolfe, Peter. *Jean Rhys*. Boston: Twayne, 1980.

Index of KM's Stories
in *Katherine Mansfield's Fiction*